EASY GUITAR
WITH NOTES & TAB

Ed Sheeran

M000169270

Cover photo: Ernesto Ruscio / Contributor / Getty Images

ISBN 978-1-4950-2186-2

HAL•LEONARD®
CORPORATION
7777 W. BLUEMOUND RD. P.O. BOX 13819 MILWAUKEE, WI 53213

Visit Hal Leonard Online at
www.halleonard.com

STRUM AND PICK PATTERNS

This chart contains the suggested strum and pick patterns that are referred to by number at the beginning of each song in this book. The symbols ⊓ and ∨ in the strum patterns refer to down and up strokes, respectively. The letters in the pick patterns indicate which right-hand fingers play which strings.

p = thumb
i = index finger
m = middle finger
a = ring finger

For example; Pick Pattern 2
is played: thumb - index - middle - ring

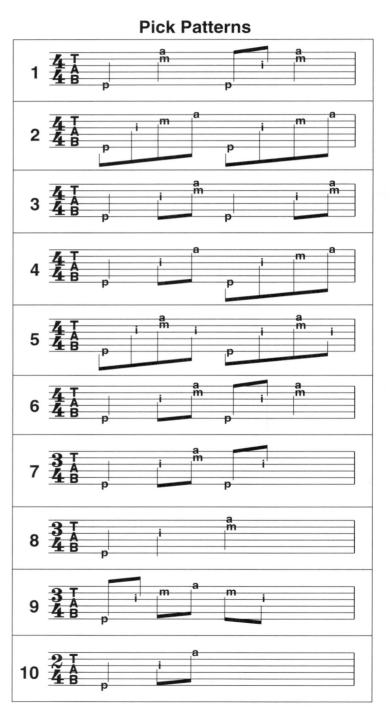

You can use the 3/4 Strum and Pick Patterns in songs written in compound meter (6/8, 9/8, 12/8, etc.). For example, you can accompany a song in 6/8 by playing the 3/4 pattern twice in each measure. The 4/4 Strum and Pick Patterns can be used for songs written in cut time (¢) by doubling the note time values in the patterns. Each pattern would therefore last two measures in cut time.

Contents

The A Team

Words and Music by Ed Sheeran

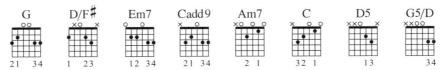

*Capo II

Strum Pattern: 3
Pick Pattern: 3

Intro
Moderately slow, in 2

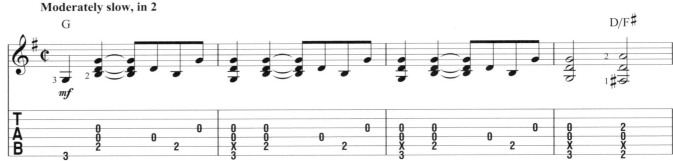

*Optional: To match recording, place capo at 2nd fret.

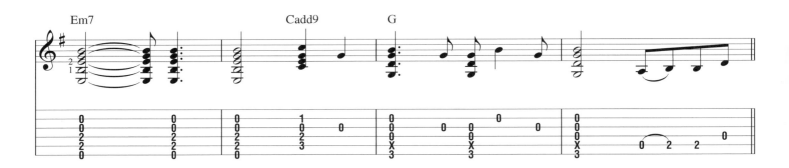

Verse

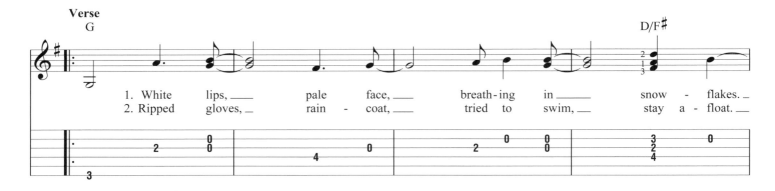

1. White lips, ___ pale face, ___ breath-ing in ___ snow - flakes.
2. Ripped gloves, _ rain - coat, _ tried to swim, _ stay a - float.

___ Burnt lungs, ___ sour taste. ___
___ Dry house, _ wet ___ clothes. _

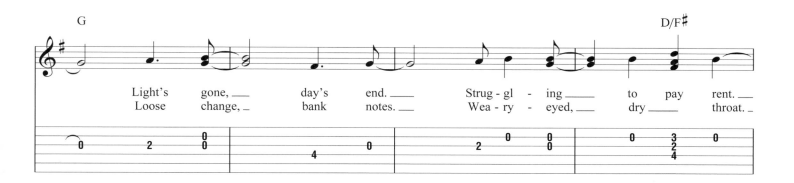

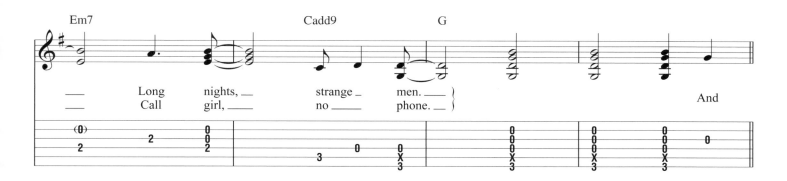

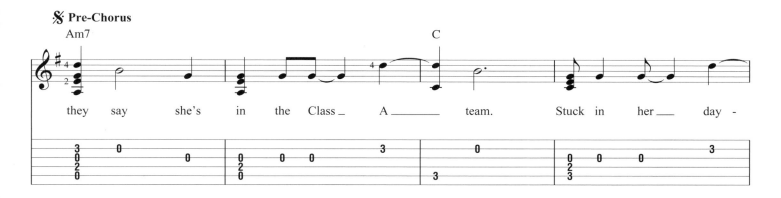

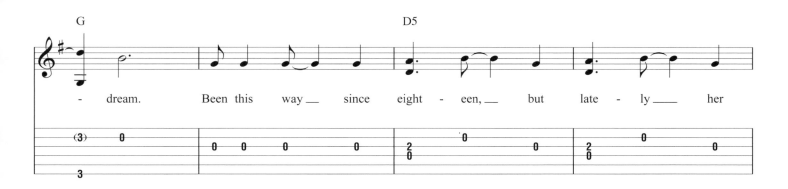

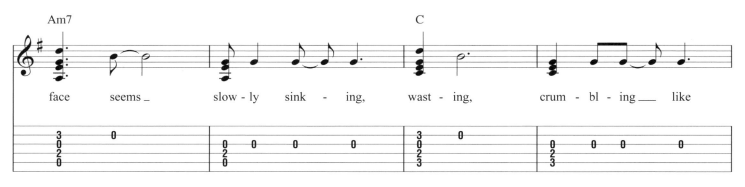

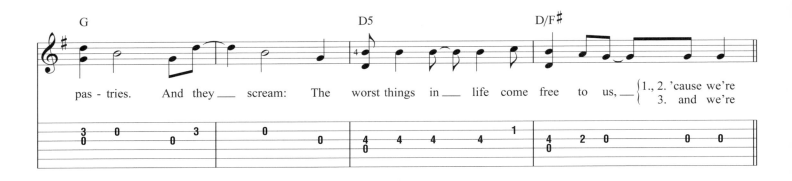

pas - tries. And they ___ scream: The worst things in ___ life come free to us, ___ { 1., 2. 'cause we're
{ 3. and we're

Chorus

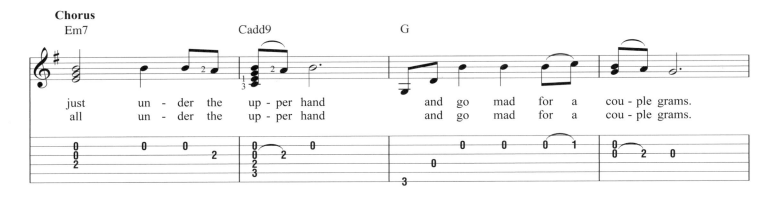

just un - der the up - per hand and go mad for a cou - ple grams.
all un - der the up - per hand and go mad for a cou - ple grams.

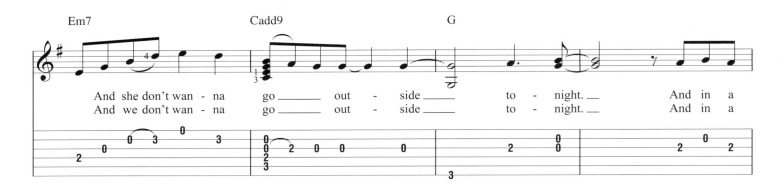

And she don't wan - na go ___ out - side ___ to - night. ___ And in a
And we don't wan - na go ___ out - side ___ to - night. ___ And in a

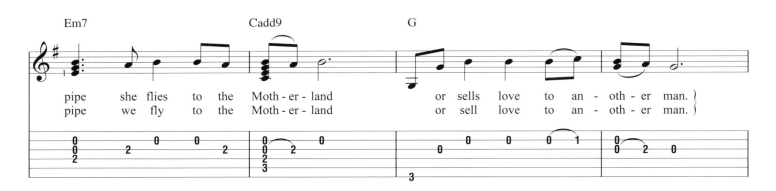

pipe she flies to the Moth - er - land or sells love to an - oth - er man. }
pipe we fly to the Moth - er - land or sell love to an - oth - er man. }

To Coda ⊕

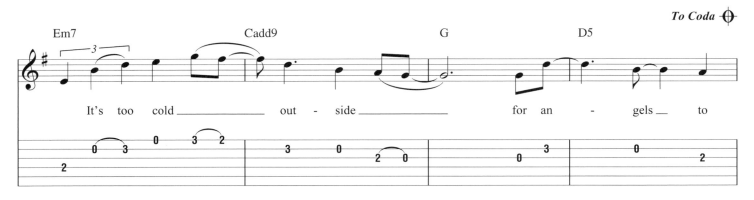

It's too cold ___ out - side ___ for an - gels ___ to

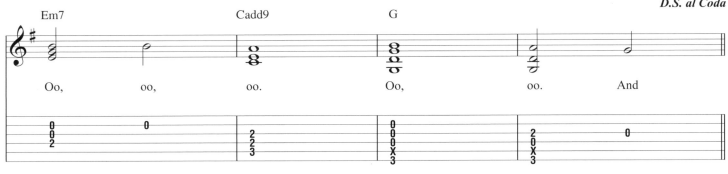

Oo,   oo,   oo.   Oo,   oo.   And

⊕ Coda

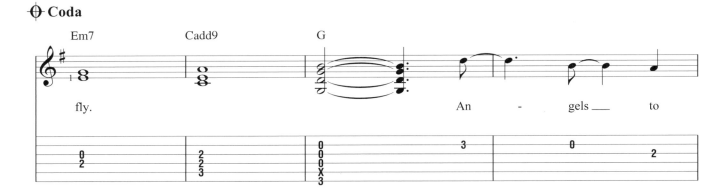

fly.   An - gels _____ to

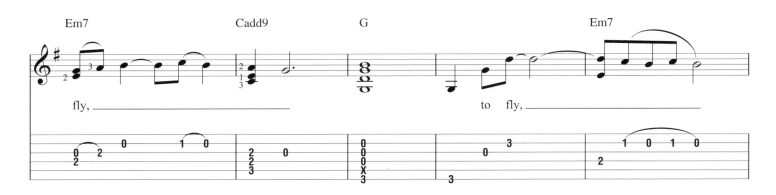

fly, _____   to   fly, _____

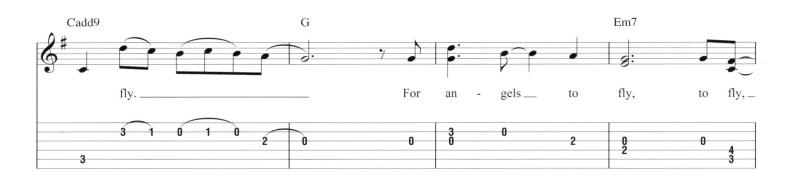

fly. _____   For   an - gels _____ to   fly,   to fly, _

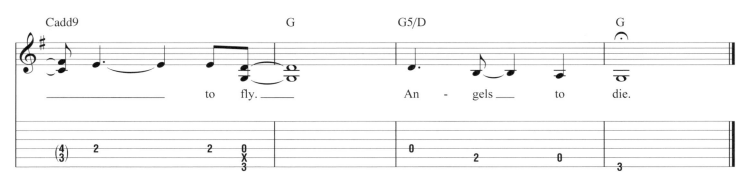

_____   to   fly. _____   An - gels _____ to   die.

8

All of the Stars

from the Motion Picture Soundtrack THE FAULT IN OUR STARS

Words and Music by Ed Sheeran and John McDaid

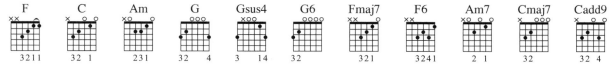

F   C   Am   G   Gsus4   G6   Fmaj7   F6   Am7   Cmaj7   Cadd9

*Tune down 1/2 step:
(low to high) Eb-Ab-Db-Gb-Bb-Eb

Strum Pattern: 2
Pick Pattern: 5

Verse

Moderately slow

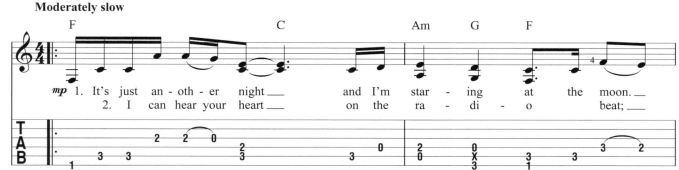

mp 1. It's just an-oth-er night ___ and I'm star-ing at the moon. ___
2. I can hear your heart ___ on the ra - di - o beat; ___

*Optional: To match recording, tune down 1/2 step.

I saw a shoot-ing star and thought of you. I sang a lull-a-by ___ by the
they're play-ing "Chas-ing Cars" and I thought of us. Back to the time ___ you were

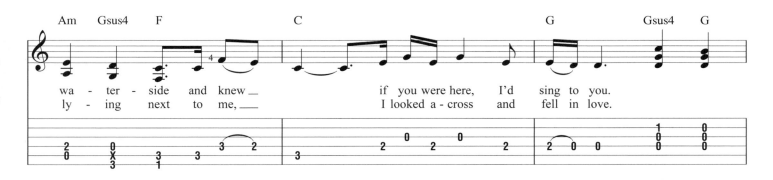

wa - ter - side and knew ___ if you were here, I'd sing to you.
ly - ing next to me, ___ I looked a - cross and fell in love.

You're on the oth - er side ___ as the sky - line splits in two, ___ miles a - way ___ from
So I took your hand ___ back through lamp - lit streets and dew, ___ ev -'ry - thing ___ led

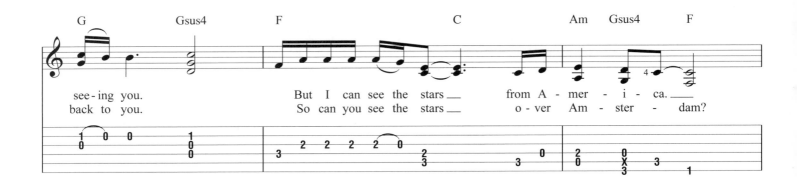

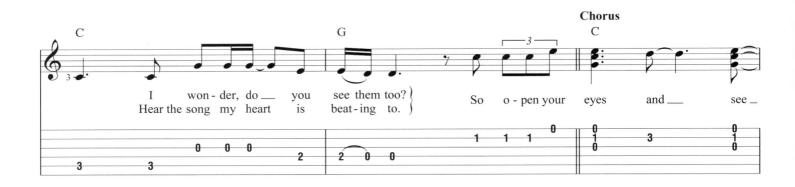

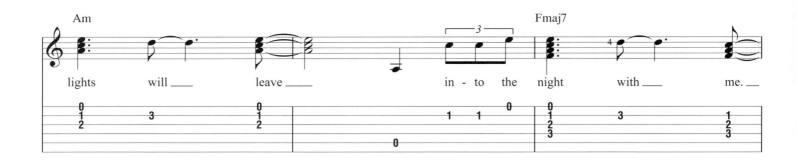

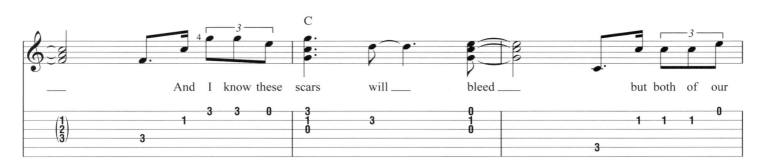

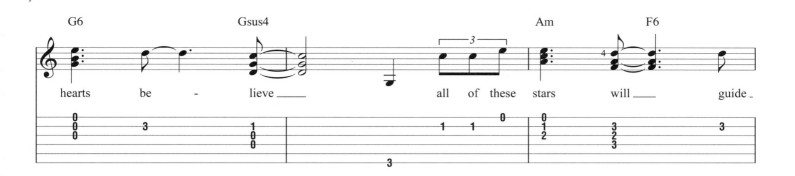

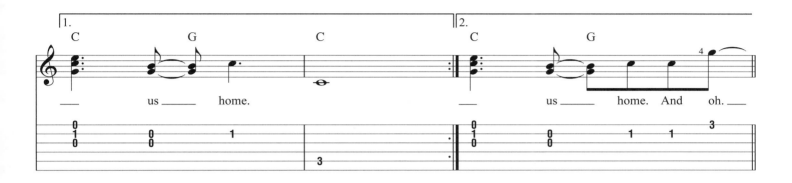

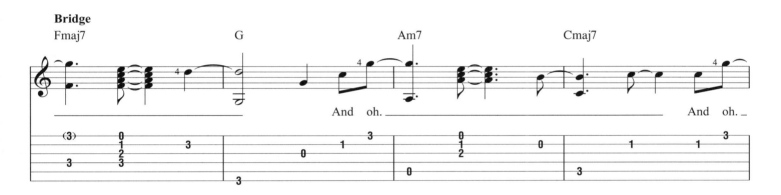

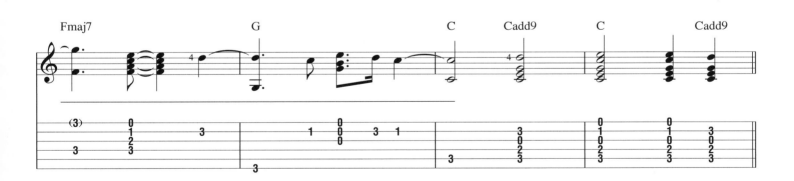

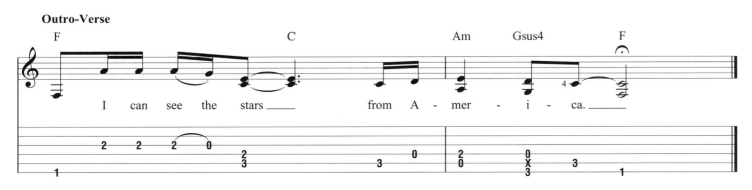

Don't

Words and Music by Ed Sheeran, Dawn Robinson, Benjamin Levin,
Raphael Saadiq, Ali Jones-Muhammad and Conesha Owens

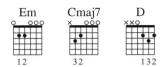

*Capo I

Strum Pattern: 3
Pick Pattern: 5

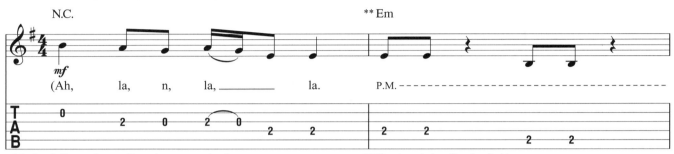

*Optional: To match recording, place capo at 1st fret.　　　　**Chord symbols reflect implied harmony.

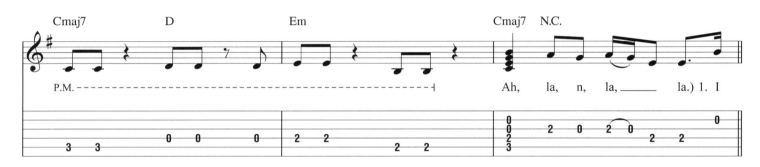

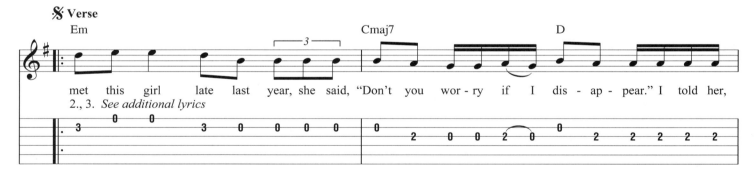

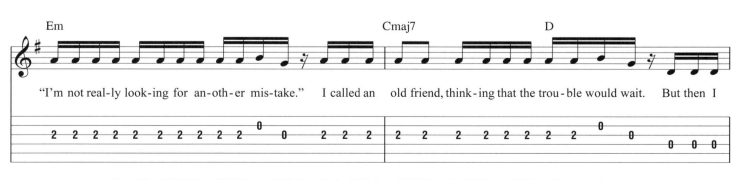

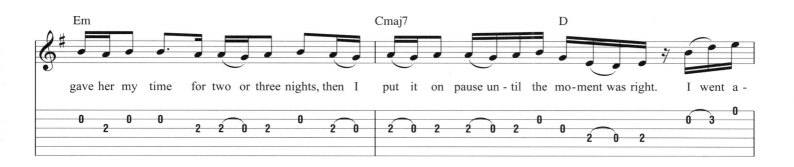

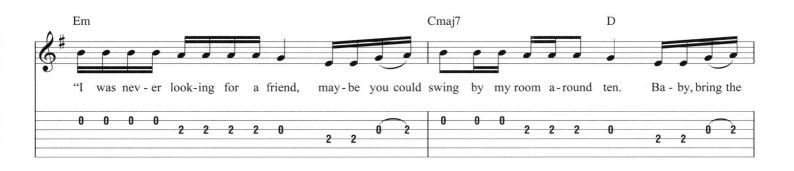

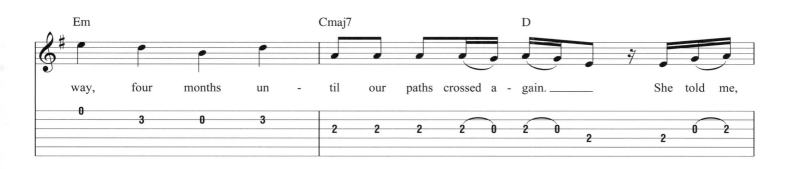

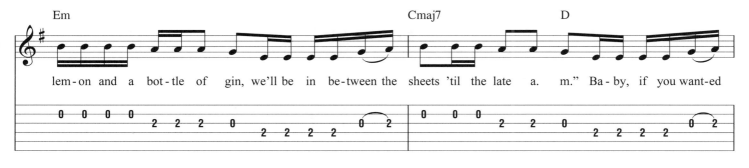

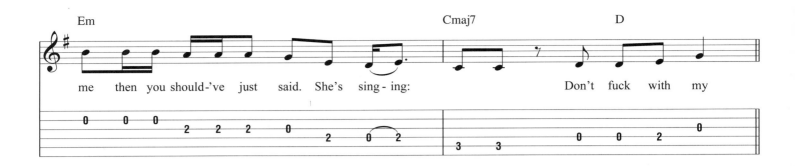

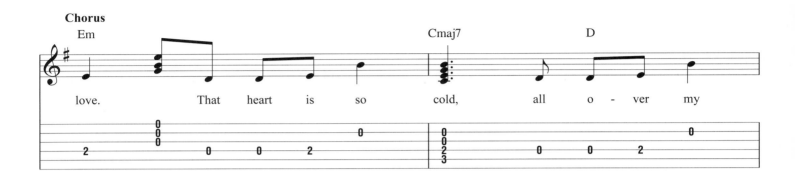

Chorus

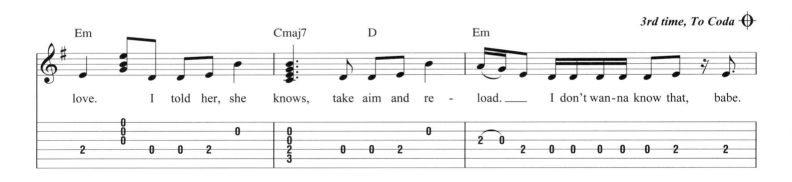

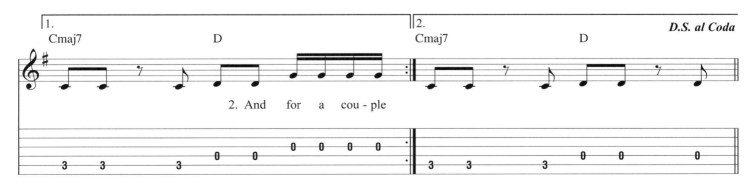

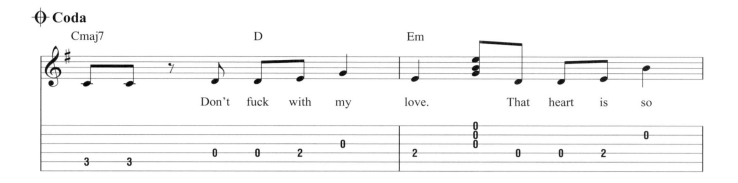

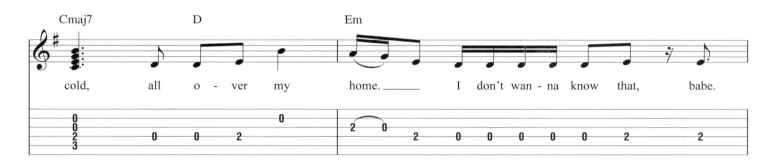

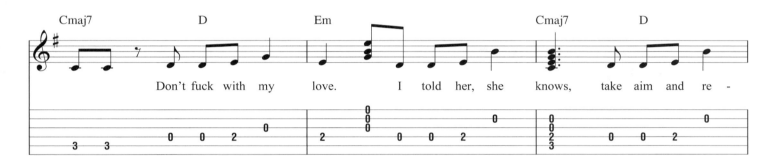

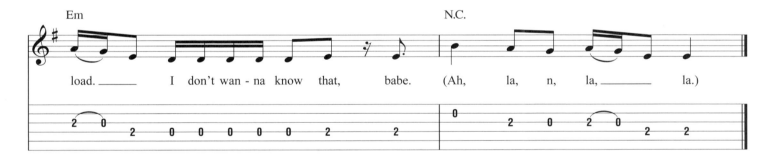

Additional Lyrics

2. And for a couple weeks I only wanna see her,
   We drink away the days with a take-away pizza.
   Before, a text message was the only way to reach her,
   Now she's staying at my place and loves the way I treat her.
   Singing out Aretha, all over the track like a feature,
   And never wants to sleep, I guess that I don't want to either.
   But me and her, we make money the same way,
   Four cities, two planes, the same day.
   And those shows have never been what it's about,
   But maybe we'll go together and just figure it out.
   I'd rather put on a film with you and sit on the couch,
   But we should get on a plane or we'll be missing it now.
   Wish I'd have written it down the way that things played out,
   When she was kissing him, how I was confused about.
   Now she should figure it out while I'm sat here singing:

3. (Knock, knock, knock) on my hotel door,
   I don't even know if she knows what for.
   She was crying on my shoulder, I already told ya,
   Trust and respect is what we do this for.
   I never intended to be next,
   But you didn't need to take him to bed, that's all.
   And I never saw him as a threat
   Until you disappeared with him to have sex, of course.
   It's not like we were both on tour,
   We were staying on the same fucking hotel floor.
   And I wasn't looking for a promise or commitment,
   But it was never just fun, and I thought you were diff'rent.
   This is not the way you realise what you wanted.
   It's a bit too much, too late if I'm honest.
   And all this time, God knows I'm singing:

Give Me Love

Words and Music by Ed Sheeran, Chris Leonard and Jake Gosling

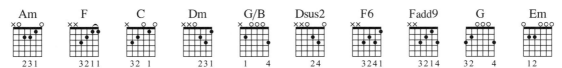

*Capo I

Strum Pattern: 7
Pick Pattern: 7

Intro
Slow, in 1

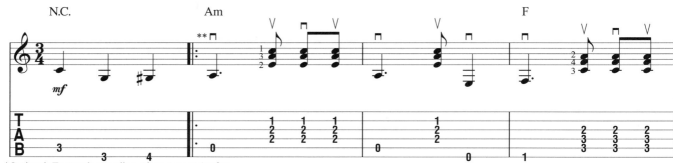

*Optional: To match recording, place capo at 1st fret.

** ⊓ = downstroke, ∨ = upstroke.

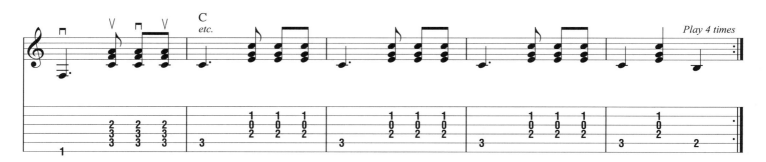

Play 4 times

% Verse

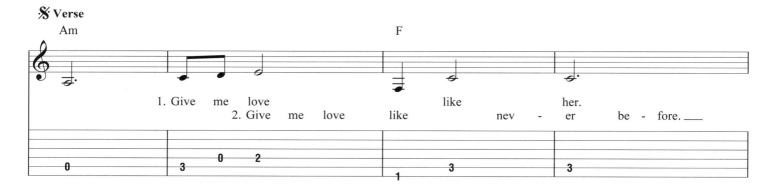

1. Give me love like her.
2. Give me love like nev - er be - fore. ___

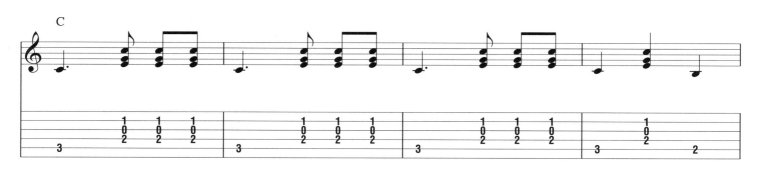

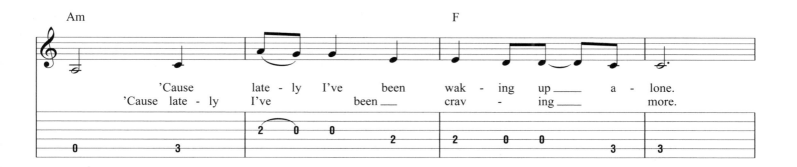
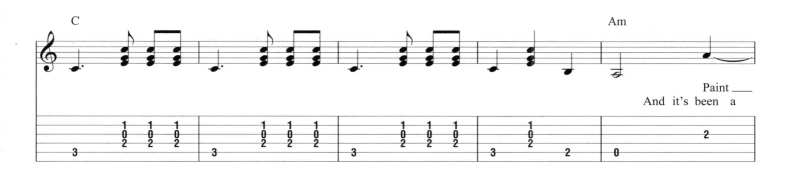
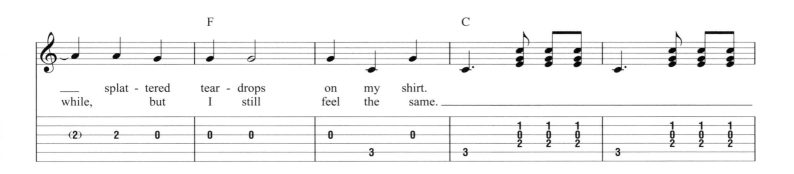
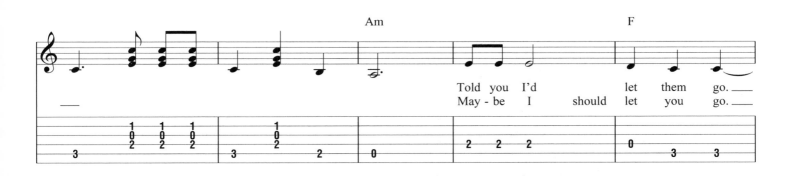
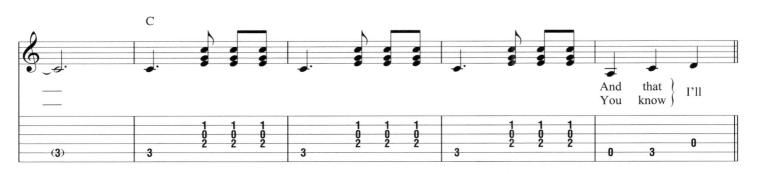

Pre-Chorus

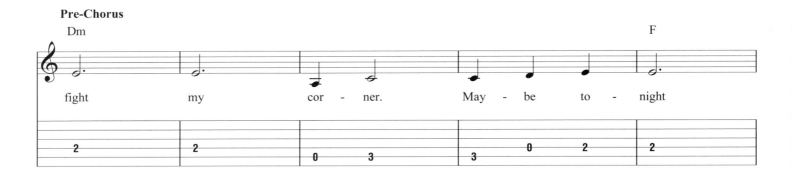

fight   my   cor - ner.   May - be to - night

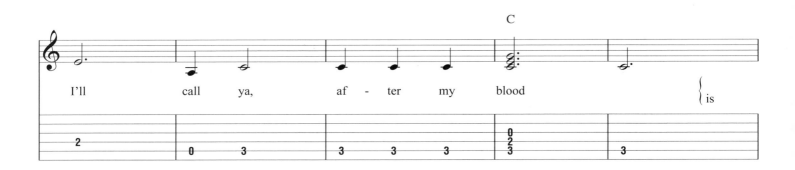

I'll   call ya,   af - ter my   blood   is

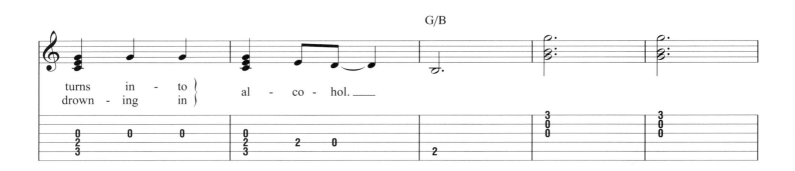

turns   in - to   al - co - hol.
drown - ing   in

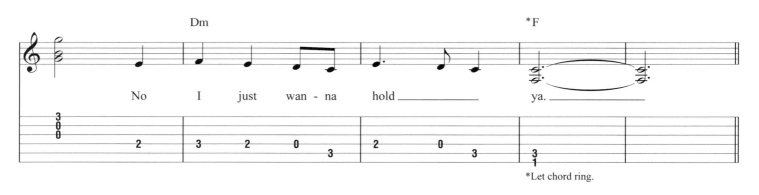

No   I   just wan - na   hold _____   ya. _____

*Let chord ring.

Chorus

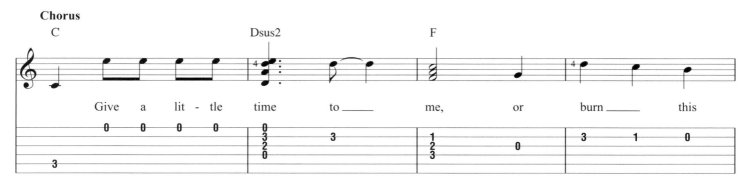

Give a lit - tle time to _____ me,   or burn _____ this

18

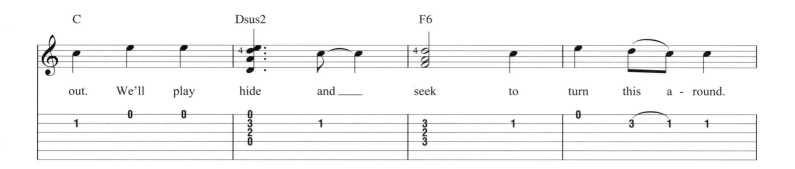

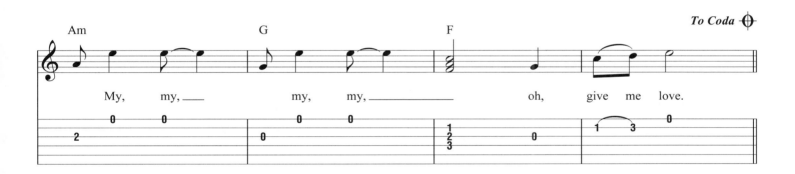

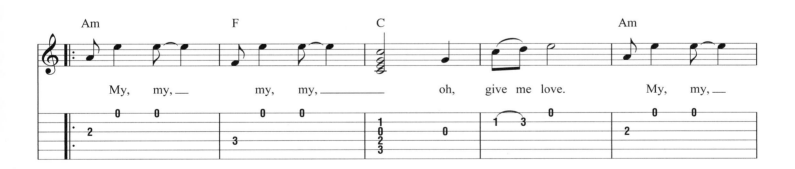

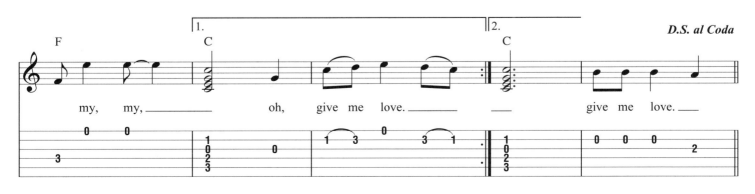

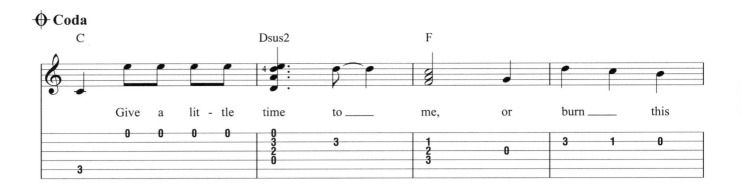

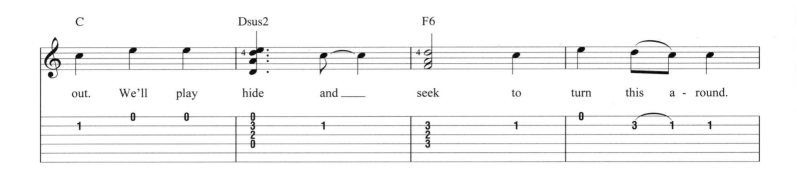

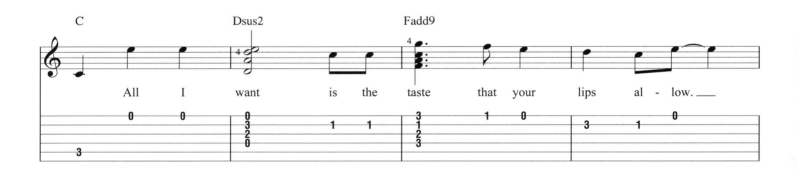

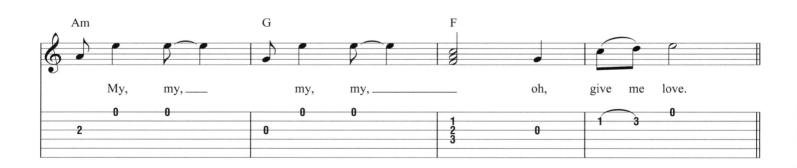

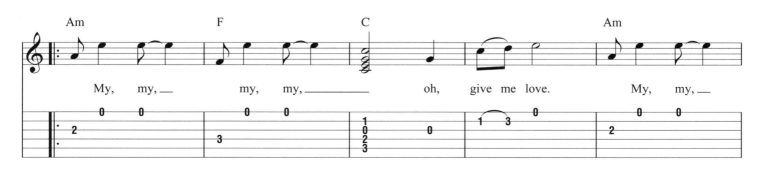

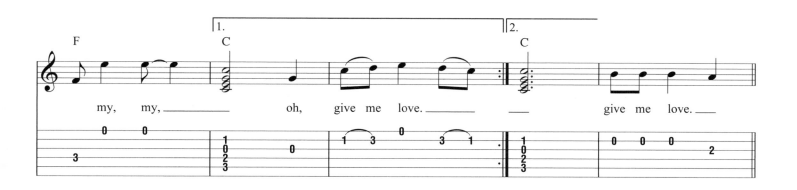

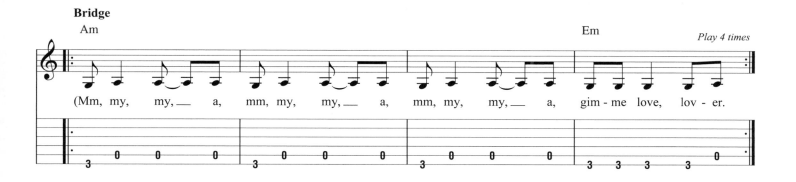

Bridge

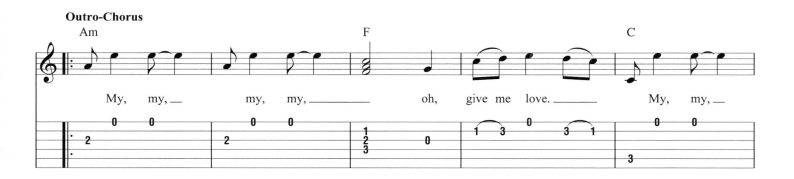

Outro-Chorus

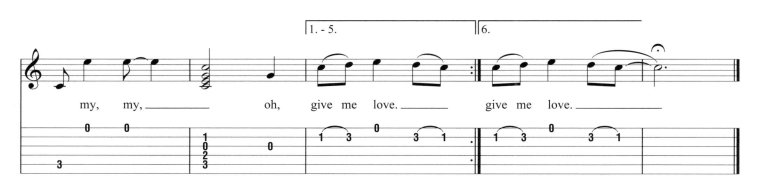

I See Fire

Words and Music by Ed Sheeran

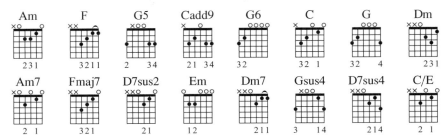

*Capo I

Strum Pattern: 6
Pick Pattern: 6

Intro
Freely

N.C.(Am)

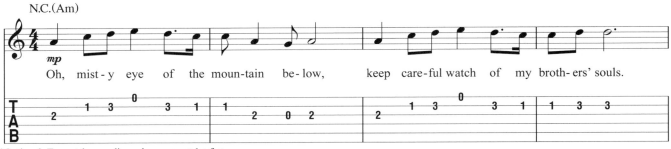

Oh, mist-y eye of the moun-tain be-low, keep care-ful watch of my broth-ers' souls.

*Optional: To match recording, place capo at 1st fret.

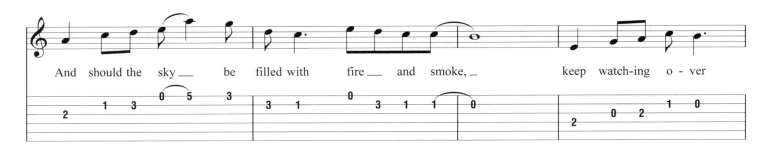

And should the sky ___ be filled with fire ___ and smoke, ___ keep watch-ing o - ver

Moderately slow

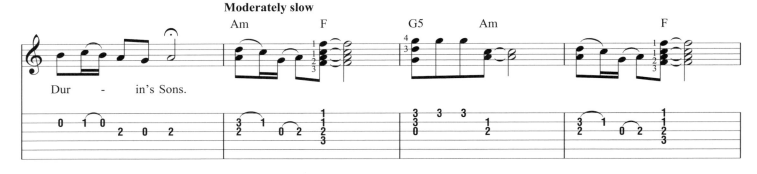

Dur - in's Sons.

Verse

1. If this is to end ___ in fire, ___ then we should all burn to - geth- er, watch the

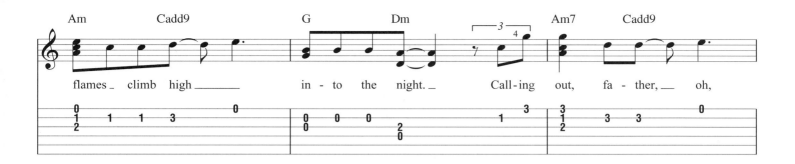

flames _ climb high _____ in - to the night. _ Call - ing out, fa - ther, _ oh,

stand by and _ we _ will watch the flames burn au - burn on the moun - tain side. _____

Verse

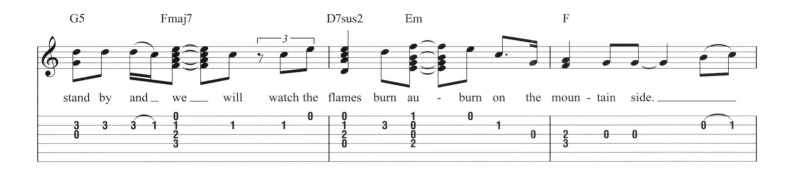

2. And if we should die to - night, _ we should
peo - ple fall, _ then sure - ly

all die to - geth - er, raise a glass _ of wine _____ for the last _ time. Call - ing
I'll do the same. Con - fined in moun - tain halls, _ we got too close to the flame. _ Call - ing

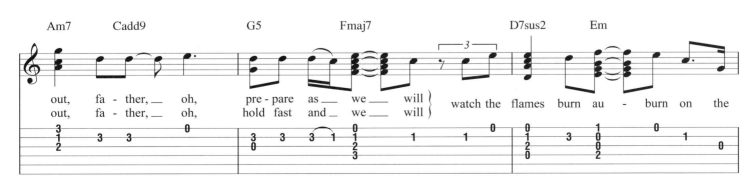

out, fa - ther, _ oh, pre - pare as _ we _ will } watch the flames burn au - burn on the
out, fa - ther, _ oh, hold fast and _ we _ will }

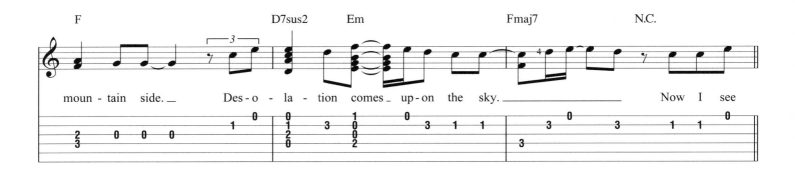

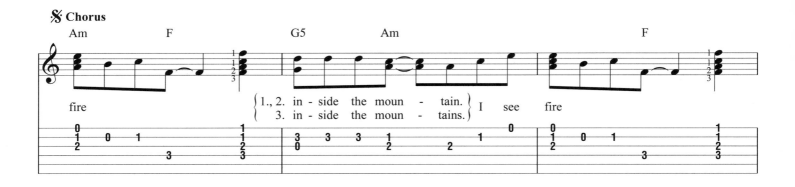

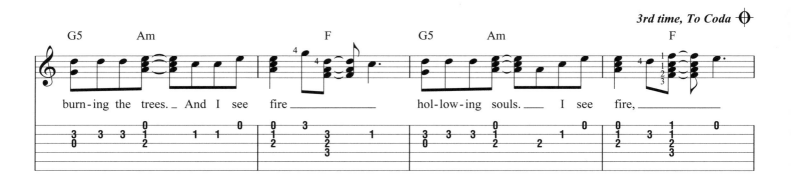

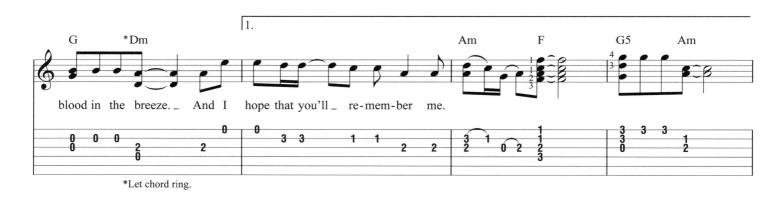

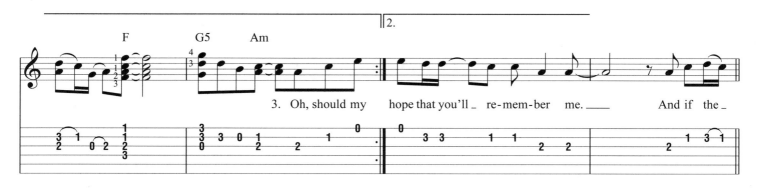

Bridge

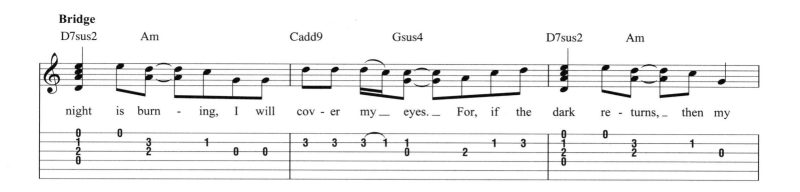

night is burn - ing, I will cov - er my ___ eyes. ___ For, if the dark re - turns, ___ then my

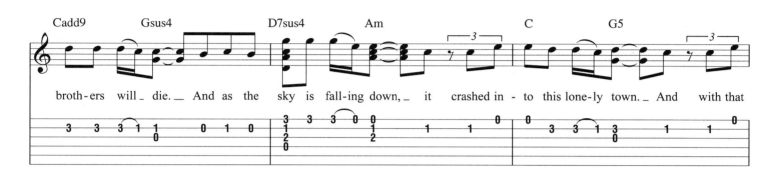

broth - ers will ___ die. ___ And as the sky is fall-ing down, ___ it crashed in - to this lone-ly town. ___ And with that

D.S. al Coda　　　　　　　　　🜙 **Coda**

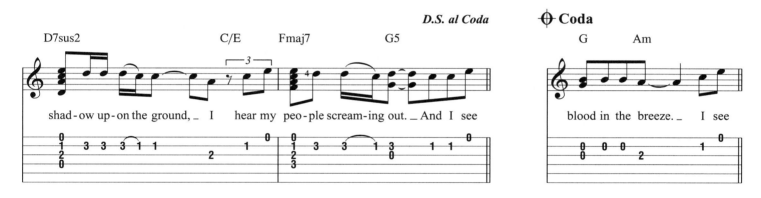

shad - ow up - on the ground, ___ I hear my peo-ple scream-ing out. ___ And I see　　　blood in the breeze. ___ I see

Outro
w/ Lead Voc. ad lib.

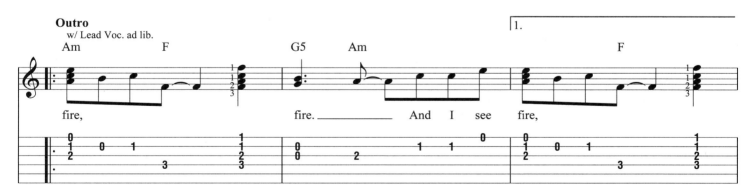

fire,　　　　fire. ___ And I see fire,

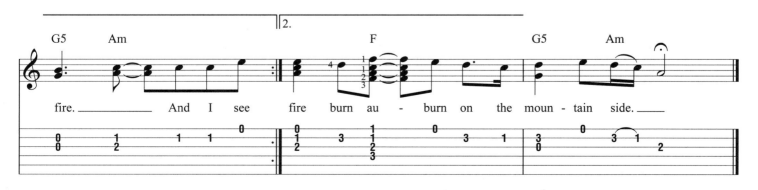

fire. ___ And I see fire burn au - burn on the moun - tain side. ___

I'm a Mess

Words and Music by Ed Sheeran

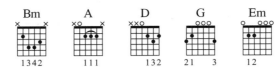

*Capo I

Strum Pattern: 6
Pick Pattern: 6

Moderately fast

Verse

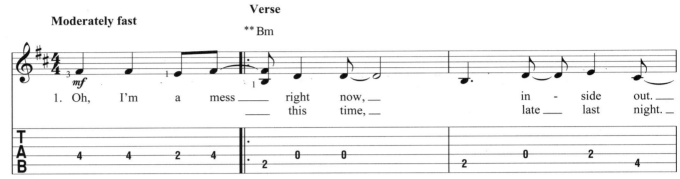

1. Oh, I'm a mess right now, in - side out.
_____ this time, _____ late _____ last night. _____

*Optional: To match recording, place capo at 1st fret.   **Chord symbols reflect implied harmony.

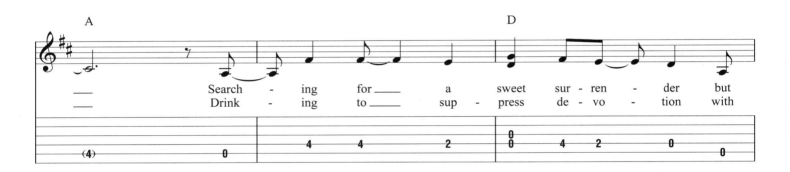

Search - ing for _____ a sweet sur - ren - der but
Drink - ing to _____ sup - press de - vo - tion with

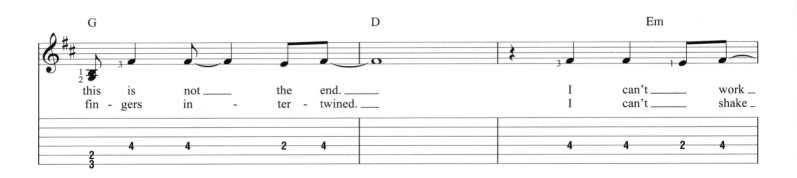

this is not _____ the end. _____ I can't _____ work
fin - gers in - ter - twined. _____ I can't _____ shake

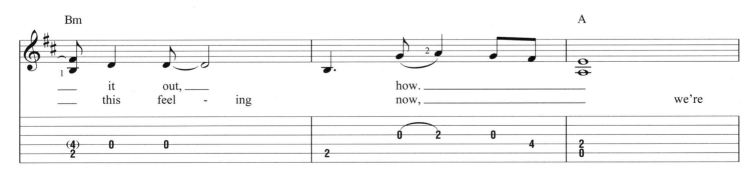

_____ it out, _____ how. _____
_____ this feel - ing now, _____ we're

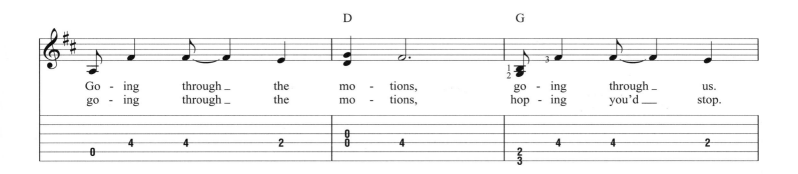

Pre-Chorus

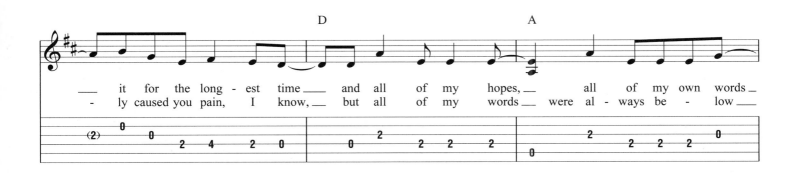

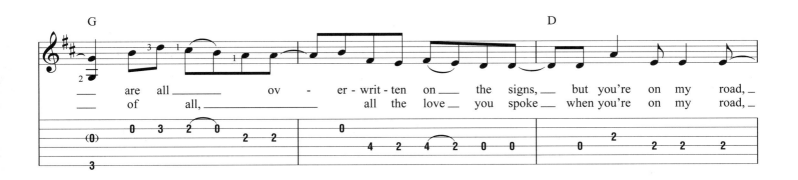

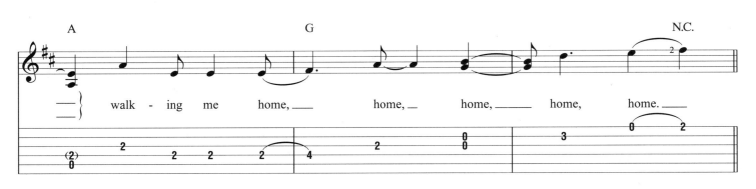

Chorus

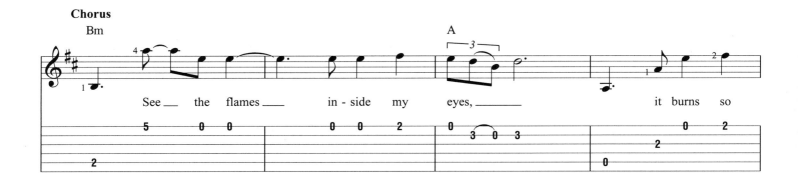

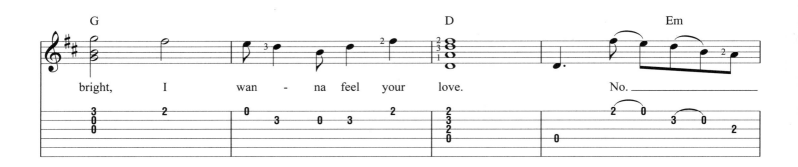

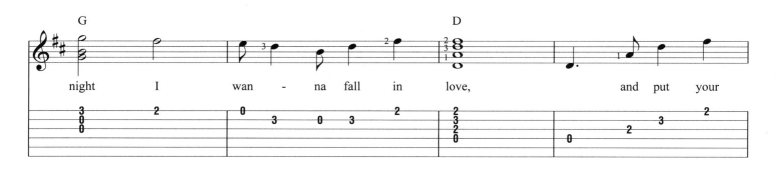

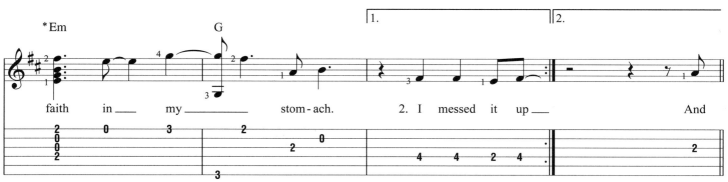

*Let chords ring, next 3 meas.

28

Outro

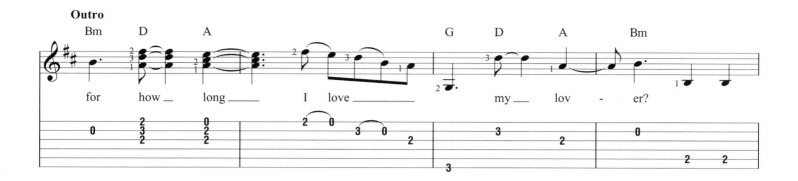

for how __ long _____ I love _____ my __ lov - er?

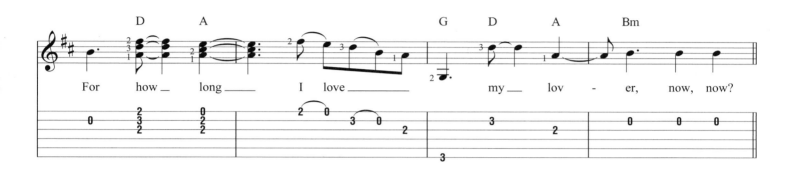

For how __ long _____ I love _____ my __ lov - er, now, now?

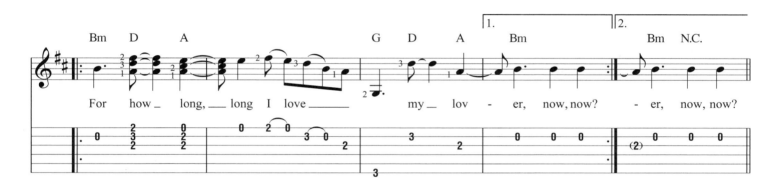

For how __ long, __ long I love _____ my __ lov - er, now, now? - er, now, now?

w/ Lead Voc. ad lib.

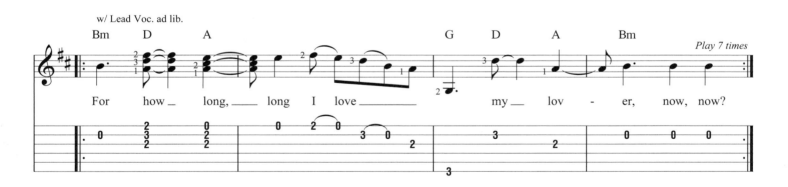

For how __ long, _____ long I love _____ my __ lov - er, now, now?

Freely

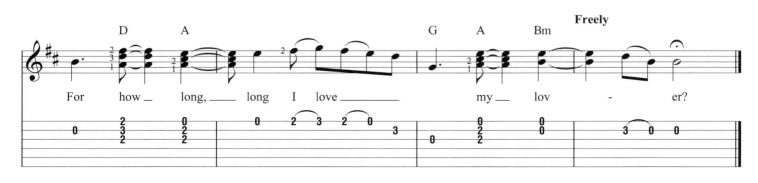

For how __ long, _____ long I love _____ my __ lov - er?

Lego House

Words and Music by Ed Sheeran, Chris Leonard and Jake Gosling

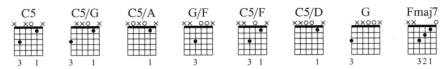

*Tune down 1/2 step:
(low to high) Eb-Ab-Db-Gb-Bb-Eb

Strum Pattern: 1
Pick Pattern: 5

Intro
Moderately slow, in 2

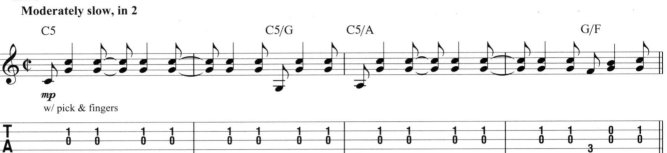

*Optional: To match recording, tune down 1/2 step.

Verse

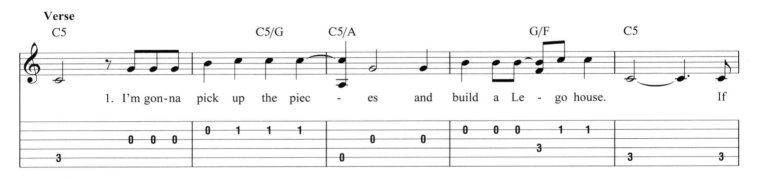

1. I'm gon-na pick up the piec -es and build a Le -go house. If

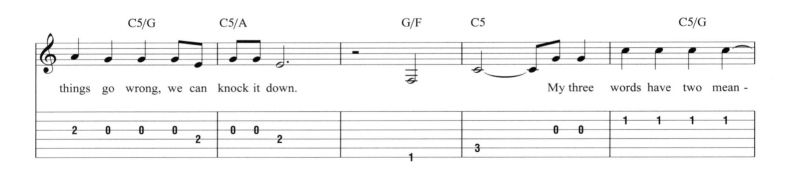

things go wrong, we can knock it down. My three words have two mean -

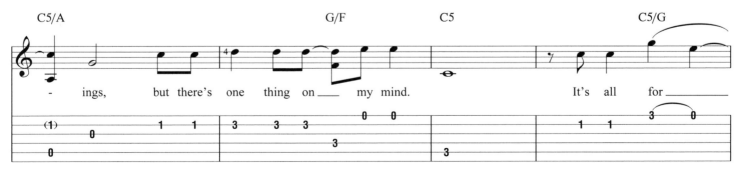

-ings, but there's one thing on ___ my mind. It's all for ___

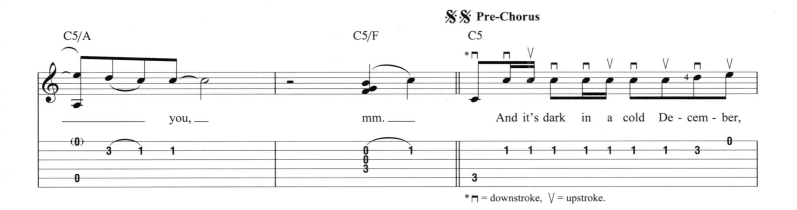

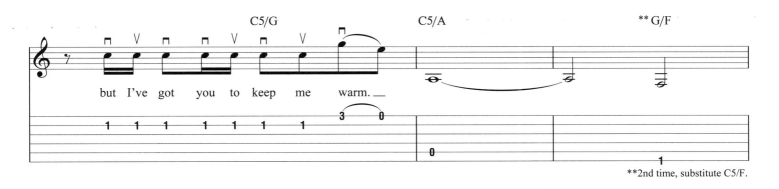

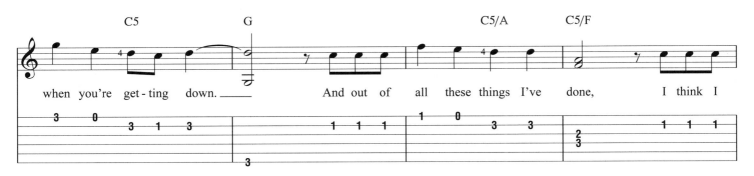

2nd time, To Coda 1 ⊕

3rd time, To Coda 2 ⊕

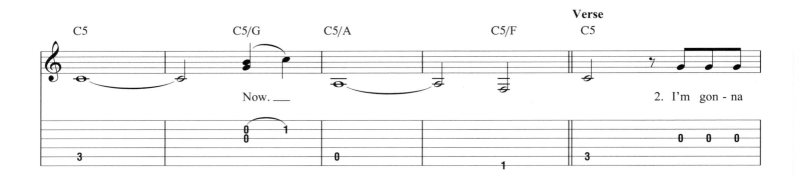

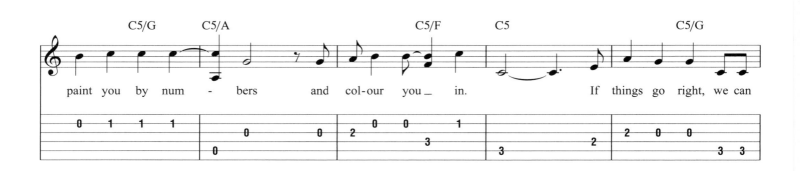

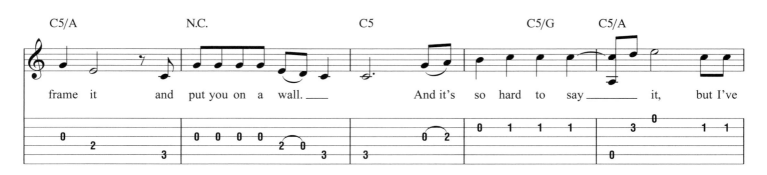

been here be - fore. _____ Now I'll sur - ren - der up __ my heart and swap it for yours. __

⊕ Coda 1

Bridge

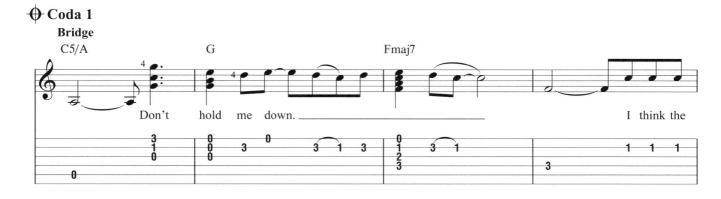

Don't hold me down. _____ I think the

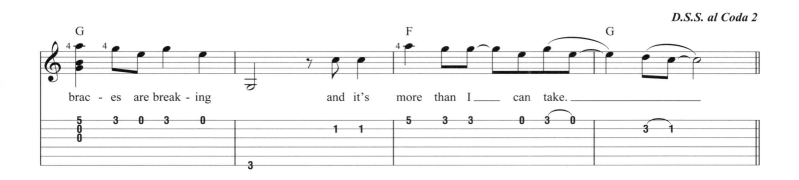

brac - es are break - ing and it's more than I ____ can take.

⊕ Coda 2

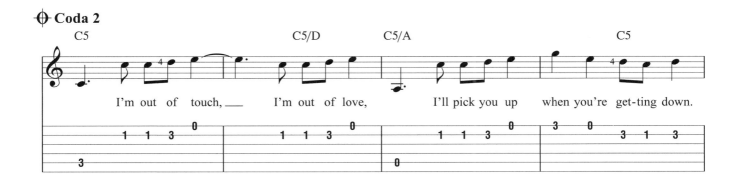

I'm out of touch, ___ I'm out of love, I'll pick you up when you're get - ting down.

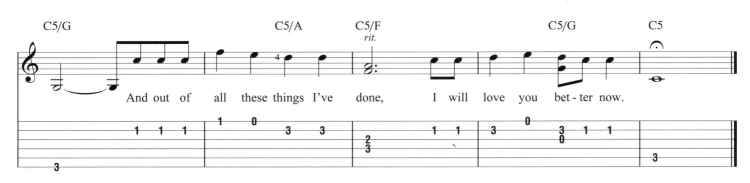

And out of all these things I've done, I will love you bet - ter now.

Photograph

Words and Music by Ed Sheeran and John McDaid

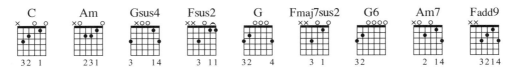

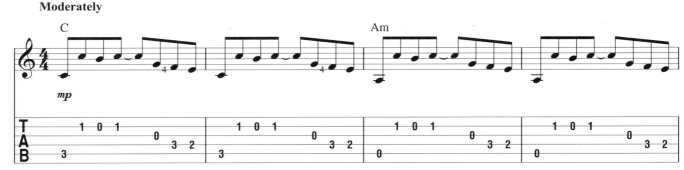

*Capo IV

Strum Pattern: 2
Pick Pattern: 6

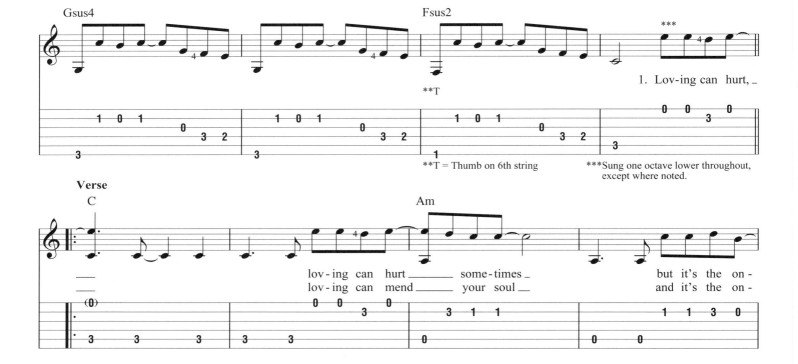

*Optional: To match recording, place capo at 4th fret.

**T = Thumb on 6th string   ***Sung one octave lower throughout, except where noted.

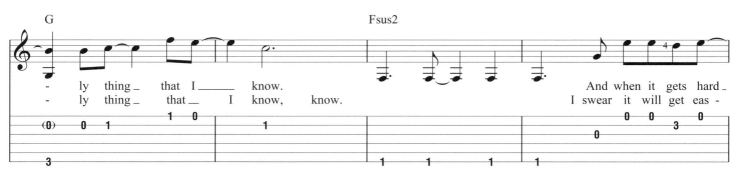

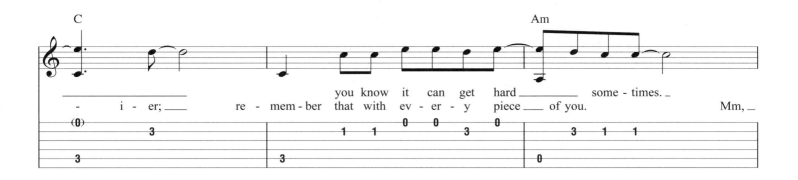

Pre-Chorus

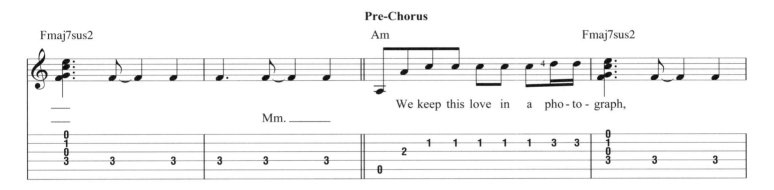

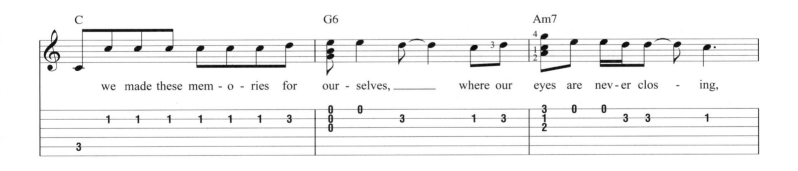

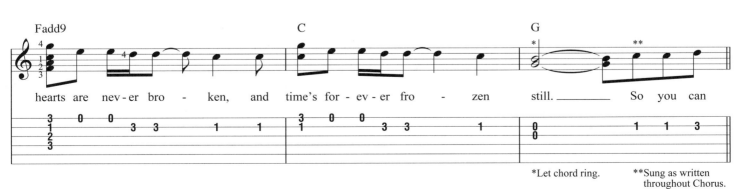

*Let chord ring. **Sung as written
throughout Chorus.

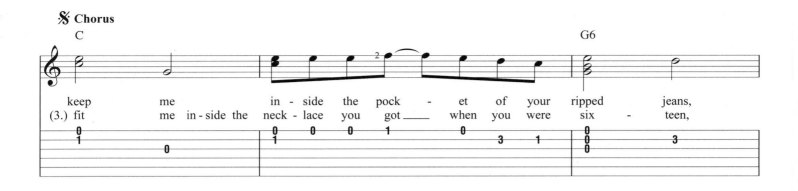

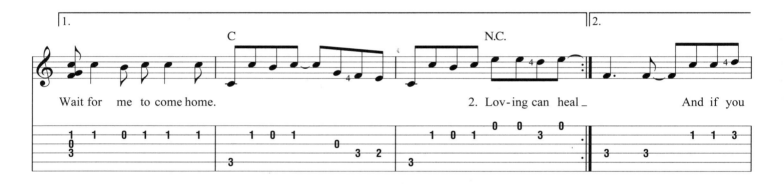

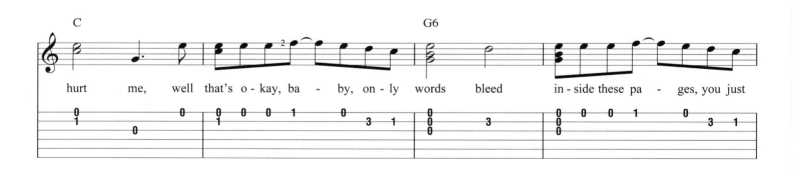

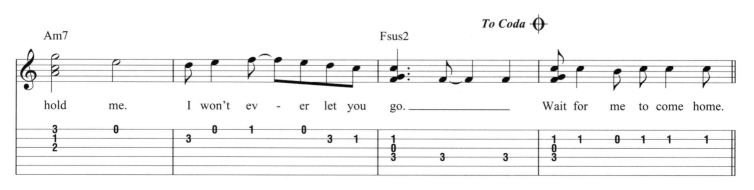

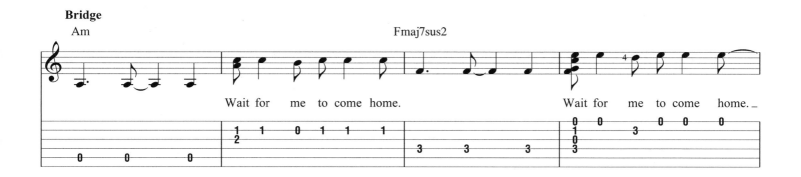

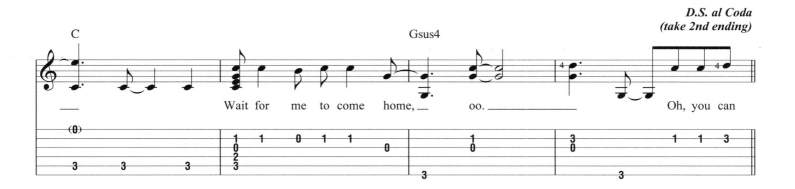

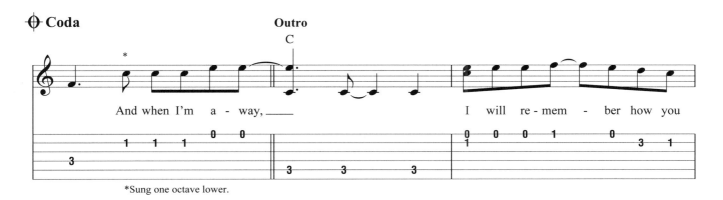

*Sung one octave lower.

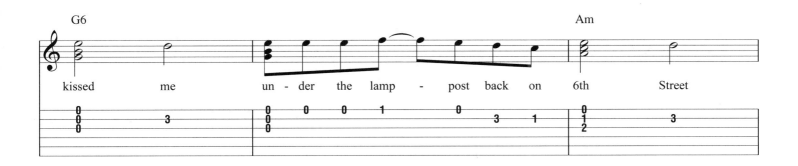

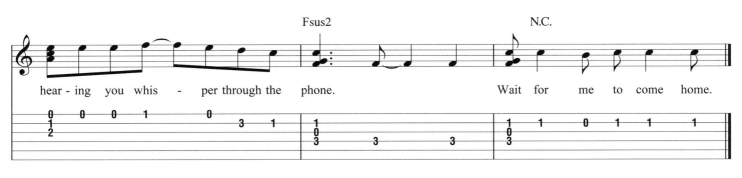

Sing

Words and Music by Ed Sheeran and Pharrell Williams

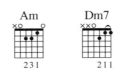

*Tune down 1/2 step:
(low to high) Eb-Ab-Db-Gb-Bb-Eb

Strum Pattern: 5
Pick Pattern: 1

Intro
Moderately

*Optional: To match recording, tune down 1/2 step.

Verse

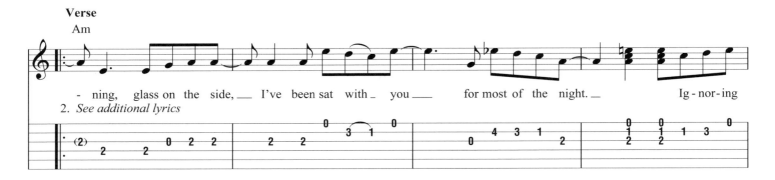

- ning, glass on the side, __ I've been sat with __ you __ for most of the night. __ Ig - nor - ing
2. *See additional lyrics*

ev - 'ry - bod - y here, __ we wish they would dis - ap - pear __ so may - be we could get down __ now. __

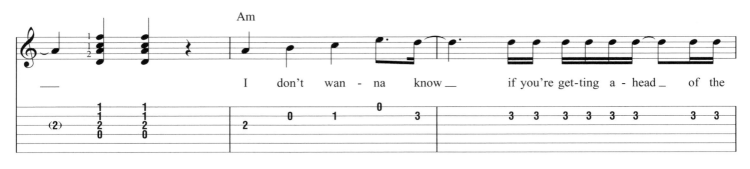

I don't wan - na know __ if you're get - ting a - head __ of the

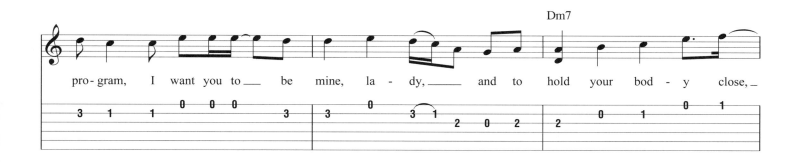

*Sung one octave higher.

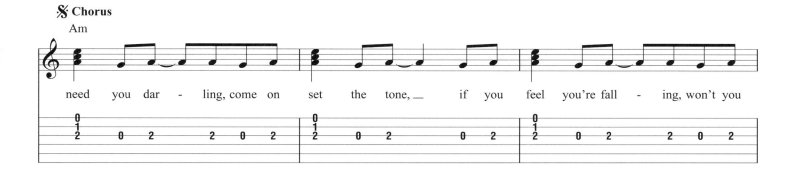

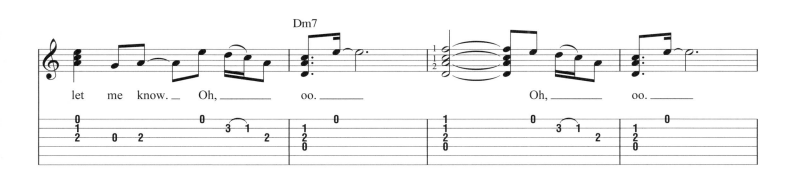

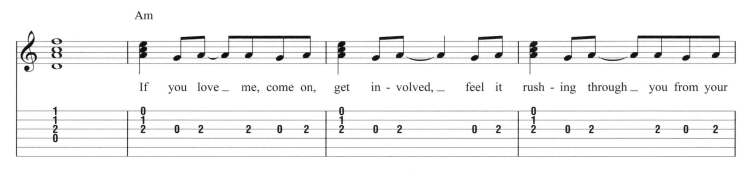

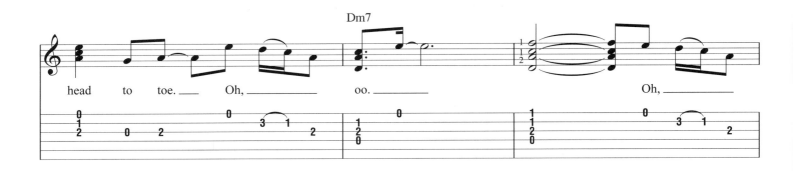

Dm7

head to toe. ___ Oh, _____ oo. _____ Oh, _____

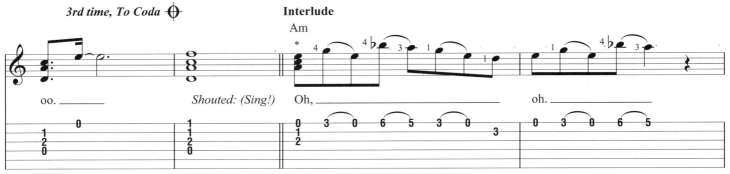

3rd time, To Coda ⊕   **Interlude**

Am

oo. _____   *Shouted: (Sing!)* Oh, _____   oh. _____

*Sung as written.

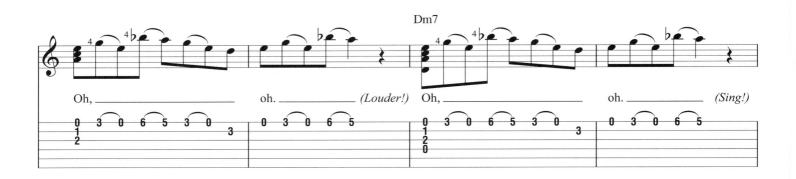

Dm7

Oh, _____ oh. _____ *(Louder!)* Oh, _____ oh. _____ *(Sing!)*

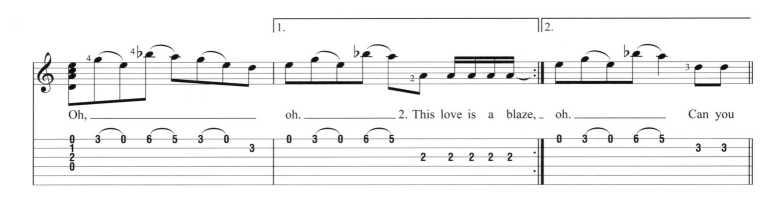

1.   2.

Oh, _____ oh. _____ 2. This love is a blaze, _ oh. _____ Can you

Bridge

Am

feel it? All the guys in here don't ev-en wan-na dance. _ Can you feel it? All that I can hear is

*Sung one octave higher.

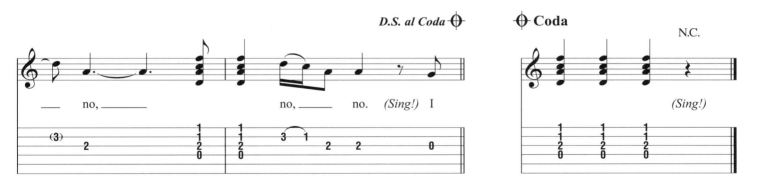

Additional Lyrics

2. This love is a blaze, I saw flames from the side of the stage
And the fire brigade comes in a couple of days.
Until then we've got nothing to say and nothing to know
But something to drink and maybe something to smoke.
Let it go until our roads are changed,
Singing, "We Found Love" in a local rave.
No, I don't really know what I'm supposed to say,
But I can just figure it out and hope and pray.
I told her my name and said, "It's nice to meet ya,"
Then she handed me a bottle of water with tequila.
I already know it, she's a keeper
Just from this one small act of kindness.
I'm in deep if anybody finds out,
I meant to drive home but I've drunk all of it now.
Not sobering up, we just sit on the couch,
One thing led to another, now she's kissing my mouth.

Tenerife Sea

Words and Music by Ed Sheeran, John McDaid and Foy Vance

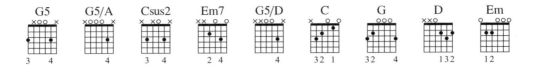

G5   G5/A   Csus2   Em7   G5/D   C   G   D   Em

*Capo I

Strum Pattern: 7
Pick Pattern: 7

Intro
Slow, in 2

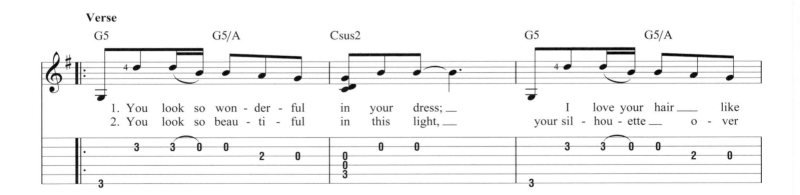

*Optional: To match recording, place capo at 1st fret.

Verse

1. You look so won-der-ful in your dress; ___ I love your hair ___ like
2. You look so beau-ti-ful in this light, ___ your sil-hou-ette ___ o-ver

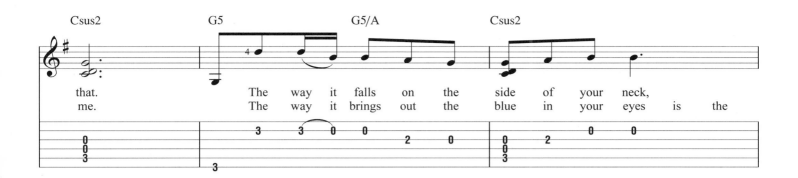

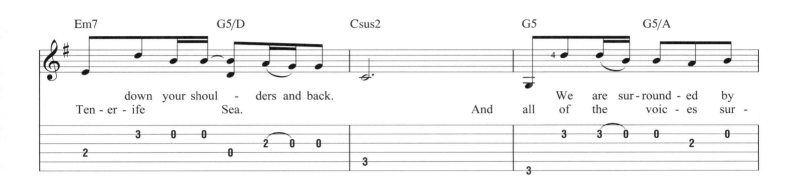

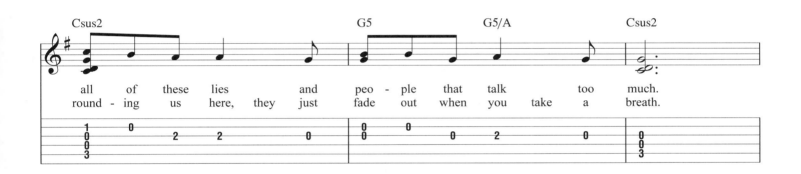

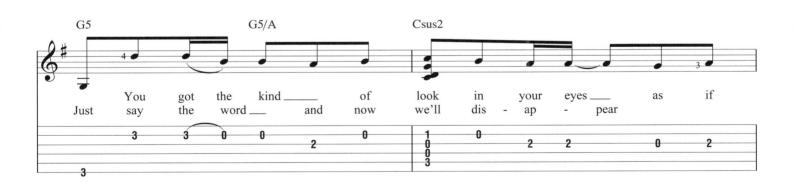

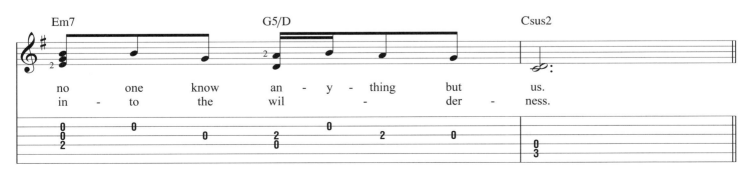

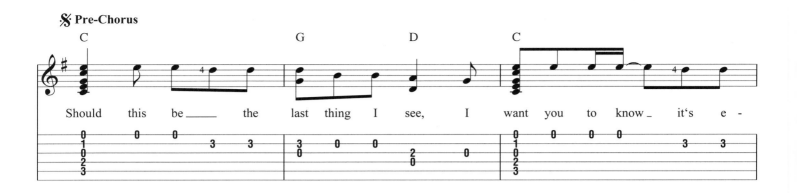

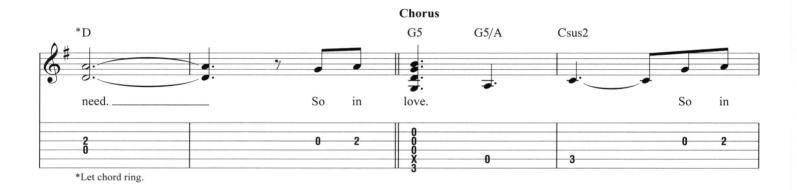

*Let chord ring.

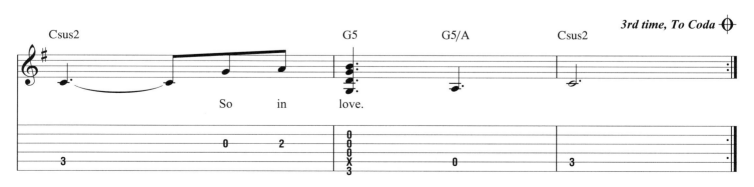

Bridge

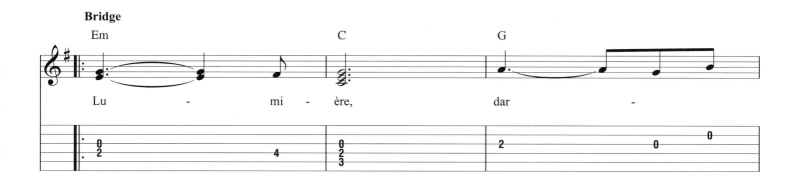

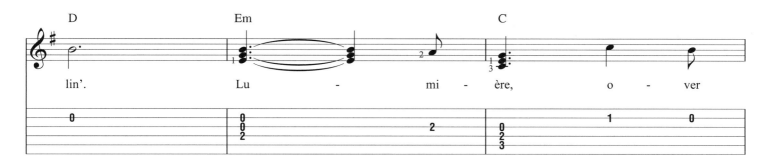

3rd time, D.S. al Coda

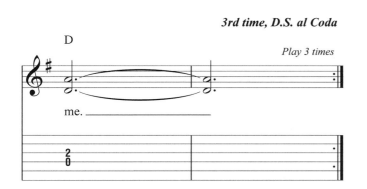

Coda
Outro-Verse

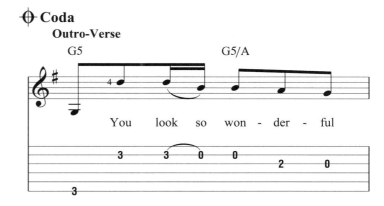

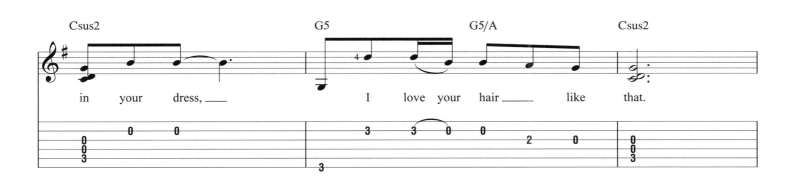

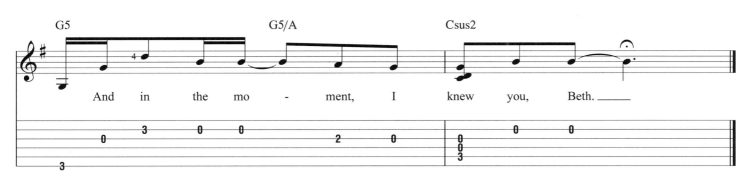

Thinking Out Loud

Words and Music by Ed Sheeran and Amy Wadge

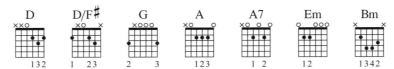

Strum Pattern: 6
Pick Pattern: 6

Verse
Moderately slow

*Chord symbols reflect implied harmony.

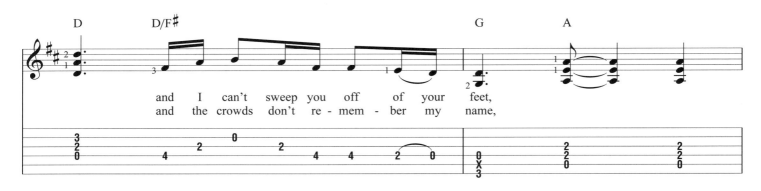

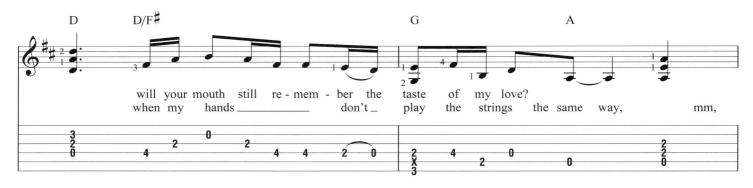

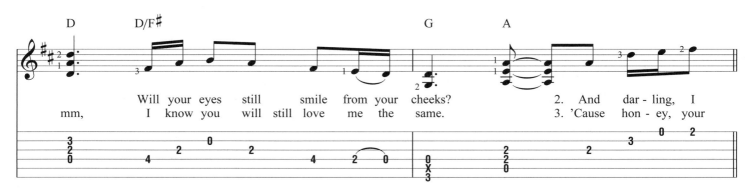

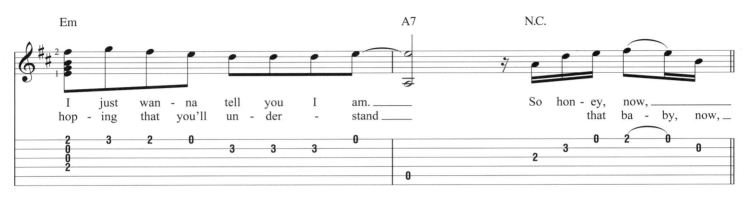

Chorus

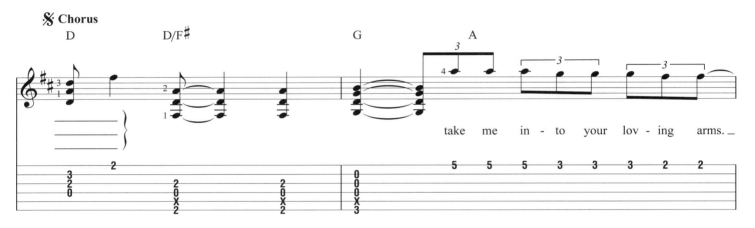

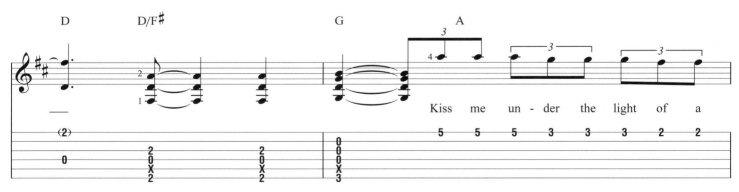

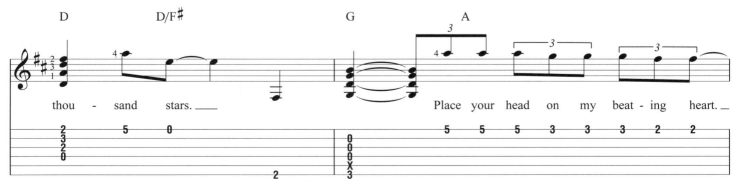

Kiss Me

Words and Music by Ed Sheeran, Julie Frost, Justin Franks and Ernest Wilson

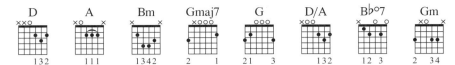

Strum Pattern: 1
Pick Pattern: 5

Intro
Moderately slow

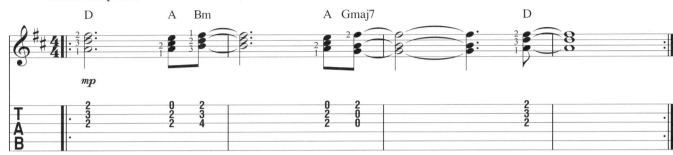

1. Set-tle down with me, ___ cov-er me up, cud-dle me ___
2. Set-tle down with me, ___ and I'll be your safe - ty, and you'll be my la -

___ in. Lie down with me, ___ yeah, and hold ___

dy. I ___ was made to keep ___ your bod-y warm, but I'm

Pre-Chorus

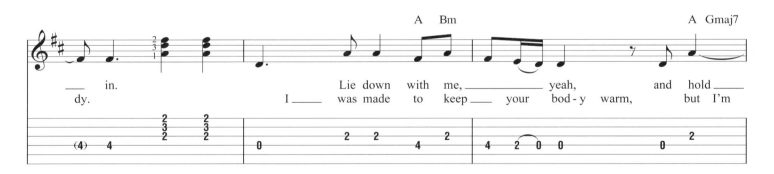

___ me in your arms. ___ And your heart's a-gainst ___ my

cold as the wind blows, so hold ___ me in your arms, ___ oh.

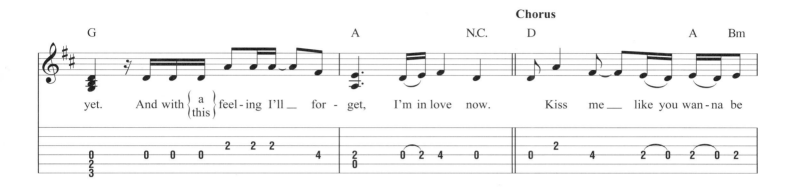

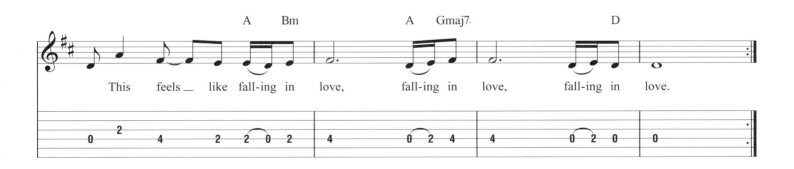

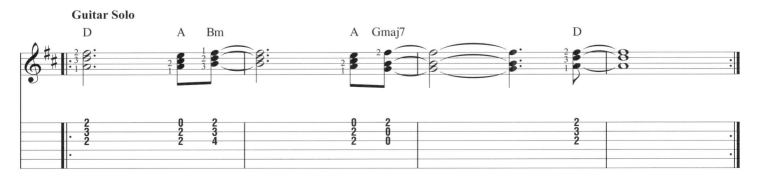

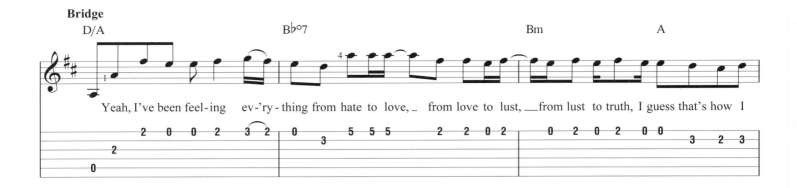

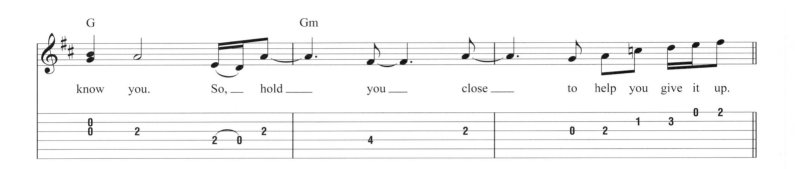

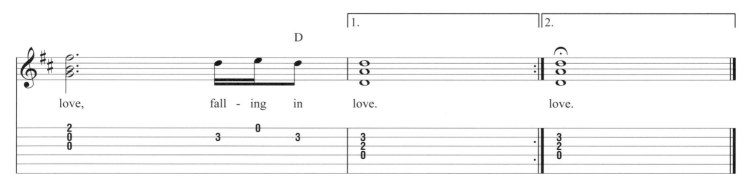

EASY GUITAR WITH NOTES & TAB

This series features simplified arrangements with notes, tab, chord charts, and strum and pick patterns.

  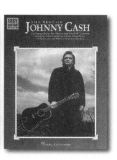

MIXED FOLIOS

00702287	Acoustic	$14.99
00702002	Acoustic Rock Hits for Easy Guitar	$12.95
00702166	All-Time Best Guitar Collection	$19.99
00699665	Beatles Best	$12.95
00702232	Best Acoustic Songs for Easy Guitar	$12.99
00119835	Best Children's Songs	$16.99
00702233	Best Hard Rock Songs	$14.99
00703055	The Big Book of Nursery Rhymes & Children's Songs	$14.99
00322179	The Big Easy Book of Classic Rock Guitar	$24.95
00698978	Big Christmas Collection	$16.95
00702394	Bluegrass Songs for Easy Guitar	$12.99
00703387	Celtic Classics	$14.99
00125023	Chart Hits of 2013-2014	$14.99
00118314	Chart Hits of 2012-2013	$14.99
00702149	Children's Christian Songbook	$7.95
00702237	Christian Acoustic Favorites	$12.95
00702028	Christmas Classics	$7.95
00101779	Christmas Guitar	$14.99
00702185	Christmas Hits	$9.95
00702141	Classic Rock	$8.95
00702203	CMT's 100 Greatest Country Songs	$27.95
00702283	The Contemporary Christian Collection	$16.99
00702006	Contemporary Christian Favorites	$9.95
00702239	Country Classics for Easy Guitar	$19.99
00702282	Country Hits of 2009–2010	$14.99
00702085	Disney Movie Hits	$12.95
00702257	Easy Acoustic Guitar Songs	$14.99
00702280	Easy Guitar Tab White Pages	$29.99
00702212	Essential Christmas	$9.95
00702041	Favorite Hymns for Easy Guitar	$9.95
00702281	4 Chord Rock	$9.99
00126894	Frozen	$14.99
00702286	Glee	$16.99
00699374	Gospel Favorites	$14.95
00122138	The Grammy Awards® Record of the Year 1958-2011	$19.99
00702160	The Great American Country Songbook	$15.99
00702050	Great Classical Themes for Easy Guitar	$6.95
00702116	Greatest Hymns for Guitar	$8.95
00702130	The Groovy Years	$9.95
00702184	Guitar Instrumentals	$9.95
00702273	Irish Songs	$12.99
00702275	Jazz Favorites for Easy Guitar	$14.99
00702274	Jazz Standards for Easy Guitar	$14.99
00702162	Jumbo Easy Guitar Songbook	$19.95
00702258	Legends of Rock	$14.99
00702261	Modern Worship Hits	$14.99
00702189	MTV's 100 Greatest Pop Songs	$24.95
00702272	1950s Rock	$14.99
00702271	1960s Rock	$14.99
00702270	1970s Rock	$14.99
00702269	1980s Rock	$14.99
00702268	1990s Rock	$14.99
00109725	Once	$14.99
00702187	Selections from O Brother Where Art Thou?	$12.95
00702178	100 Songs for Kids	$12.95
00702515	Pirates of the Caribbean	$12.99
00702125	Praise and Worship for Guitar	$9.95
00702155	Rock Hits for Guitar	$9.95
00702285	Southern Rock Hits	$12.99
00702866	Theme Music	$12.99
00121535	30 Easy Celtic Guitar Solos	$14.99
00702220	Today's Country Hits	$9.95
00702198	Today's Hits for Guitar	$9.95
00121900	Today's Women of Pop & Rock	$14.99
00702217	Top Christian Hits	$12.95
00103626	Top Hits of 2012	$14.99
00702294	Top Worship Hits	$14.99
00702206	Very Best of Rock	$9.95
00702255	VH1's 100 Greatest Hard Rock Songs	$27.99
00702175	VH1's 100 Greatest Songs of Rock and Roll	$24.95
00702253	Wicked	$12.99

ARTIST COLLECTIONS

00702267	AC/DC for Easy Guitar	$15.99
00702598	Adele for Easy Guitar	$14.99
00702001	Best of Aerosmith	$16.95
00702040	Best of the Allman Brothers	$14.99
00702865	J.S. Bach for Easy Guitar	$12.99
00702169	Best of The Beach Boys	$12.99
00702292	The Beatles — 1	$19.99
00125796	Best of Chuck Berry	$14.99
00702201	The Essential Black Sabbath	$12.95
02501615	Zac Brown Band — The Foundation	$16.99
02501621	Zac Brown Band — You Get What You Give	$16.99
00702043	Best of Johnny Cash	$16.99
00702291	Very Best of Coldplay	$12.99
00702263	Best of Casting Crowns	$12.99
00702090	Eric Clapton's Best	$10.95
00702086	Eric Clapton — from the Album Unplugged	$10.95
00702202	The Essential Eric Clapton	$12.95
00702250	blink-182 — Greatest Hits	$12.99
00702053	Best of Patsy Cline	$10.95
00702229	The Very Best of Creedence Clearwater Revival	$14.99
00702145	Best of Jim Croce	$14.99
00702278	Crosby, Stills & Nash	$12.99
00702219	David Crowder*Band Collection	$12.95
14042809	Bob Dylan	$14.99
00702276	Fleetwood Mac — Easy Guitar Collection	$14.99
00130952	Foo Fighters	$14.99
00139462	The Very Best of Grateful Dead	$14.99
00702136	Best of Merle Haggard	$12.99
00702227	Jimi Hendrix — Smash Hits	$14.99
00702288	Best of Hillsong United	$12.99
00702236	Best of Antonio Carlos Jobim	$12.95
00702245	Elton John — Greatest Hits 1970–2002	$14.99
00129855	Jack Johnson	$14.99
00702204	Robert Johnson	$9.95
00702234	Selections from Toby Keith — 35 Biggest Hits	$12.95
00702003	Kiss	$9.95
00110578	Best of Kutless	$12.99
00702216	Lynyrd Skynyrd	$15.99
00702182	The Essential Bob Marley	$12.95
00702346	Bruno Mars — Doo-Wops & Hooligans	$12.99
00121925	Bruno Mars – Unorthodox Jukebox	$12.99
00702248	Paul McCartney — All the Best	$14.99
00702129	Songs of Sarah McLachlan	$12.95
00125484	The Best of MercyMe	$12.99
02501316	Metallica — Death Magnetic	$15.95
00702209	Steve Miller Band — Young Hearts (Greatest Hits)	$12.95
00124167	Jason Mraz	$14.99
00702096	Best of Nirvana	$14.99
00702211	The Offspring — Greatest Hits	$12.95
00138026	One Direction	$14.99
00702030	Best of Roy Orbison	$12.95
00702144	Best of Ozzy Osbourne	$14.99
00702279	Tom Petty	$12.99
00102911	Pink Floyd	$16.99
00702139	Elvis Country Favorites	$9.95
00702293	The Very Best of Prince	$12.99
00669415	Best of Queen for Guitar	$14.99
00109279	Best of R.E.M.	$14.99
00702208	Red Hot Chili Peppers — Greatest Hits	$12.95
00702093	Rolling Stones Collection	$17.95
00702196	Best of Bob Seger	$12.95
00702252	Frank Sinatra — Nothing But the Best	$12.99
00702010	Best of Rod Stewart	$14.95
00702049	Best of George Strait	$12.95
00702259	Taylor Swift for Easy Guitar	$14.99
00702260	Taylor Swift — Fearless	$12.99
00139727	Taylor Swift — 1989	$16.99
00115960	Taylor Swift — Red	$16.99
00702290	Taylor Swift — Speak Now	$15.99
00702262	Chris Tomlin Collection	$14.99
00702226	Chris Tomlin — See the Morning	$12.95
00702427	U2 — 18 Singles	$14.99
00102711	Van Halen	$16.99
00702108	Best of Stevie Ray Vaughan	$10.95
00702123	Best of Hank Williams	$12.99
00702111	Stevie Wonder — Guitar Collection	$9.95
00702228	Neil Young — Greatest Hits	$15.99
00119133	Neil Young — Harvest	$14.99
00702188	Essential ZZ Top	$10.95

Prices, contents and availability subject to change without notice.

HAL•LEONARD® CORPORATION
7777 W. BLUEMOUND RD. P.O. BOX 13819 MILWAUKEE, WI 53213

Visit Hal Leonard online at
www.halleonard.com

0315

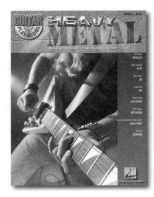

This series will help you play your favorite songs quickly and easily. Just follow the tab and listen to the CD or online audio to hear how the guitar should sound, and then play along using the separate backing tracks. Mac or PC users can also slow down the tempo without changing pitch by using the CD in their computer. The melody and lyrics are included in the book so that you can sing or simply follow along.

HAL•LEONARD® CORPORATION
7777 W. BLUEMOUND RD. P.O. BOX 13819 MILWAUKEE, WI 53213

For complete songlists, visit Hal Leonard online at
www.halleonard.com

Prices, contents, and availability subject to change without notice.

0315

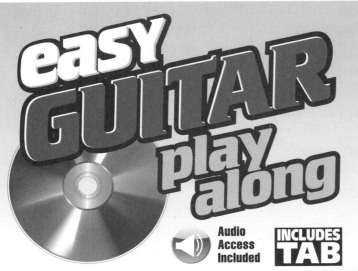

easy GUITAR play along

The *Easy Guitar Play Along*® Series features streamlined transcriptions of your favorite songs. Just follow the tab, listen to the audio to hear how the guitar should sound, and then play along using the backing tracks. The CD is playable on any CD player, and is also enhanced to include the Amazing Slowdowner technology so Mac and PC users can adjust the recording to any tempo without changing the pitch!

Audio Access Included

INCLUDES TAB

1. ROCK CLASSICS
Jailbreak • Living After Midnight • Mississippi Queen • Rocks Off • Runnin' Down a Dream • Smoke on the Water • Strutter • Up Around the Bend.
00702560 Book/CD Pack....... $14.99

2. ACOUSTIC TOP HITS
About a Girl • I'm Yours • The Lazy Song • The Scientist • 21 Guns • Upside Down • What I Got • Wonderwall.
00702569 Book/CD Pack....... $14.99

3. ROCK HITS
All the Small Things • Best of You • Brain Stew (The Godzilla Remix) • Californication • Island in the Sun • Plush • Smells like Teen Spirit • Use Somebody.
00702570 Book/CD Pack....... $14.99

4. ROCK 'N' ROLL
Blue Suede Shoes • I Get Around • I'm a Believer • Jailhouse Rock • Oh, Pretty Woman • Peggy Sue • Runaway • Wake up Little Susie.
00702572 Book/CD Pack..... $14.99

5. ULTIMATE ACOUSTIC
Against the Wind • Babe, I'm Gonna Leave You • Come Monday • Free Fallin' • Give a Little Bit • Have You Ever Seen the Rain? • New Kid in Town • We Can Work It Out.
00702573 Book/CD Pack........ $14.99

6. CHRISTMAS SONGS
Have Yourself a Merry Little Christmas • A Holly Jolly Christmas • The Little Drummer Boy • Run Rudolph Run • Santa Claus Is Comin' to Town • Silver and Gold • Sleigh Ride • Winter Wonderland.
00101879 Book/CD Pack......... $14.99

7. BLUES SONGS FOR BEGINNERS
Come On (Part 1) • Double Trouble • Gangster of Love • I'm Ready • Let Me Love You Baby • Mary Had a Little Lamb • San-Ho-Zay • T-Bone Shuffle.
00103235 Book/CD Pack..... $14.99

8. ACOUSTIC SONGS FOR BEGINNERS
Barely Breathing • Drive • Everlong • Good Riddance (Time of Your Life) • Hallelujah • Hey There Delilah • Lake of Fire • Photograph.
00103240 Book/CD Pack..... $14.99

9. ROCK SONGS FOR BEGINNERS
Are You Gonna Be My Girl • Buddy Holly • Everybody Hurts • In Bloom • Otherside • The Rock Show • Santa Monica • When I Come Around.
00103255 Book/CD Pack..... $14.99

10. GREEN DAY
Basket Case • Boulevard of Broken Dreams • Good Riddance (Time of Your Life) • Holiday • Longview • 21 Guns • Wake Me up When September Ends • When I Come Around.
00122322 Book/CD Pack..... $14.99

11. NIRVANA
All Apologies • Come As You Are • Heart Shaped Box • Lake of Fire • Lithium • The Man Who Sold the World • Rape Me • Smells like Teen Spirit.
00122325 Book/CD Pack $14.99

12. TAYLOR SWIFT
Fifteen • Love Story • Mean • Picture to Burn • Red • We Are Never Ever Getting Back Together • White Horse • You Belong with Me.
00122326 Book/CD Pack $16.99

14. JIMI HENDRIX – SMASH HITS
All Along the Watchtower • Can You See Me • Crosstown Traffic • Fire • Foxey Lady • Hey Joe • Manic Depression • Purple Haze • Red House • Remember • Stone Free • The Wind Cries Mary.
00130591 Book/Online Audio........ $24.99

HAL•LEONARD® CORPORATION
7777 W. BLUEMOUND RD. P.O. BOX 13819 MILWAUKEE, WI 53213

www.halleonard.com

Prices, contents, and availability subject to change without notice.

O315